Praise for *Habits of High Performers*

'In the quest for excellence, mindset is everything. Learn from a seven-times world champion turned elite coach how to cultivate the leadership qualities that command victory. This book is your ticket to the inner circle of high performers' Scott O'Neil, CEO of LIV Golf and former CEO of the Philadelphia 76ers NBA team

'A profound exploration of the personal journey to leadership excellence, offering insights and strategies that resonate with anyone looking to lead themselves and others with authenticity and impact' Jim Keyes, former CEO of 7-Eleven

'James gets to the heart of what it means to lead. It's not about titles or trophies; it's about hard work, resilience, and the courage to be yourself. It's an inspiring read for anyone who wants to gain that high-performance edge' Sir John Key GNZM AC, former Prime Minister of New Zealand

'A must-read for those seeking to enhance their leadership and performance' Sam Whitelock, former New Zealand All Black

'The journey to becoming number one is as much about leading oneself as it is about skill and strategy. James's book distils the essence of this journey, offering invaluable insights into the personal leadership that defines champions, making it a phenomenal guide for seasoned and aspiring leaders' Jason Stacy, mindset and performance coach for world number-one tennis professional Aryna Sabalenka

'A powerful work that decodes how the very best do it' Robin Sharma, number-one worldwide bestselling author of *The 5 AM Club*

'*Habits of High Performers* is a compelling guide to excelling in both life and work. James delivers powerful insights and hands-on tips for anyone who is striving to be their best, personally and professionally. Thought provoking, inspiring and practical, it's a must-read masterclass in personal leadership!' Karen Pflug, CSO of Ingka Group – IKEA

'With a compelling blend of personal anecdotes and evidence-based strategies, James equips readers with tools to transform their approach to personal development. This book is a treasure trove of wisdom for those aspiring to craft a life of fulfillment and excellence beyond the conventional metrics of success' Nabeela Elsayed, former COO of Walmart Canada

'James captures the essence of what it takes to triumph in today's competitive landscape. Drawing on rich lessons from the arenas of elite sports and global business, he provides clear, actionable strategies that anyone can implement to elevate their performance to world-class levels. This book is a must-read for those serious about redefining success and achieving their best, offering a powerful blend of inspiration and practical advice' Zion Armstrong, former President of Adidas North America

'This book is a game-changer. James Laughlin's *Habits of High Performers* delivers the clarity and tools needed to achieve sustainable success in both life and leadership. It's a compelling and indispensable read' Vahan Yepremyan, co-founder and COO of Ketchup Entertainment

'This book is a masterclass in mindset. James combines deep insight with real-world tools to help you build unshakeable inner strength and lasting success' Dr Haley Perlus, sport and performance psychologist and author of *Personal Podium*

'James Laughlin takes the science of habits and shows how it works in the real world of elite performance. Built to help people change for good, this is a rare book – rooted in evidence, rich in insight, and ready to make a real impact' Dr Gina Cleo, adjunct professor at Bond University and author of *The Habit Revolution*

'*Habits of High Performers* is a roadmap to excellence. By authoring this life-changing book, James actually displays the very characteristics of outstanding performance that he writes about. He clearly lives the strategies that he uncovers within. Not everyone can be a world champion, but there is nothing stopping you from adopting the habits of one' Sir Wayne Smith, former head coach of the Black Ferns and assistant coach of the All Blacks

'James's book offers the antidote to the scatter and overwhelm so many of us are experiencing. Whether by designer or by default, we all perform. The truth is, most of us major in minor parts of life, in an environment that seems intent on making us attention starved. *Habits of High Performers* organises a set of timeless truths for clarity and authentic fulfilment. Once you see them, it becomes impossible to neglect your commitment to pursuing your own long game. Pick up a highlighter, roll up your sleeves and give this book your full attention. The gains are cumulative and essential'
Dr Alia Bojilova, former lead psychologist of New Zealand SAS and author of *The Resilience Toolkit*

James Laughlin is an international number one bestselling author and world-renowned strategist in high-performance leadership and personal mastery. He coaches government leaders, Fortune-level CEOs, and professional athletes, helping them build the clarity, resilience, and discipline required to perform at the highest level under sustained pressure.

A seven-time world champion musician and history-making team leader, James brings lived experience of elite performance into every engagement. His work sits at the intersection of mindset, mental skills, and execution, translating possibilitarian thinking into practical results across business, sport, and public leadership.

James is the host of the *Habits of High Performers* podcast, where he interviews world political leaders, Fortune 500 CEOs, and top performers to distil the habits, decisions, and behaviours that separate the best from the rest.

Find out more at www.jjlaughlin.com

HABITS OF HIGH PERFORMERS

Essential principles to thrive in life and work

James Laughlin

Published by Maison Vero
3002 Dow Avenue, Suite 112
Tustin, CA 92780

Copyright © 2025 by JJ Laughlin Ltd

Maison Vero is a professional publishing house that partners with rising authors to bring their thought leadership to the world. By respecting the copyright of an author's intellectual property, you enable Maison Vero and the author to continue publishing exceptional books for years to come. We thank you for supporting the author's copyright by purchasing an authorized edition of this book.

No amount of this book may be reproduced or stored in any format, nor may it be uploaded to any website, database, language-learning model, or other repository, retrieval, or artificial intelligence system without express permission. All rights reserved.

Inquiries may be directed to: Maison Vero, 3002 Dow Avenue, Suite 112, Tustin, CA 92780, or info@graymilleragency.com.

For information about special discounts for bulk purchases, please call (949) 333-4872 or email info@graymilleragency.com.

Maison Vero is a partner brand of The Gray + Miller Agency, a speaking, literary, and talent consortium.

For more information on the talent represented by The Gray + Miller Agency, or to bring any of our thought leaders to your organization or live event, please visit our website at graymilleragency.com

First published September 2025 by HarperCollinsPublishers (New Zealand) Limited

Cover Design by Josh Beggs
Typeset in Adobe Garamond Pro by Kirby Jones
Author photograph by Martha Grieve

Manufactured in the United States of America

Paperback 978-1-969508-26-4
Hardcover 978-1-969508-27-1

*Caroline and Finn, you make life extraordinary.
You're the best part of my story.*

Contents

Introduction — 1

1: Get Radically Clear — 11
Principle 1: Always play the long game — 16
Principle 2: Make time for what's most important (WMI) — 21
Principle 3: Values make the vision — 33
Principle 4: Diluting your priorities will dilute your results — 41
Principle 5: Get out of your head and onto the page — 55

2: Supercharge Your Belief Systems — 69
Principle 6: Achieving begins with believing — 70
Principle 7: You're full of BS — 80
Principle 8: Beliefs separate the great from the greatest — 82
Principle 9: Seeing is believing — 92
Principle 10: GOATs focus on their strengths — 102

3: Lead Your Life on Purpose — 109
Principle 11: Do work that matters — 113
Principle 12: When your why is clear, your how is easy — 117
Principle 13: Purpose is the high performer's edge — 125

4: Multiply Your Motivation — 139
Principle 14: Desire is to a result what fuel is to a fire — 141
Principle 15: Success is an inside job — 145

Principle 16: Master your needs, master your life   150

Principle 17: High performance is hormonal   156

Principle 18: Clarity precedes action   168

5: Do the Work   **173**

Principle 19: Discipline the inner domain to dominate the outer domain   174

Principle 20: What you say, you become   178

Principle 21: High performers aren't busy   185

Principle 22: Successful people say no, a lot   194

6: Focus on Your Priorities   **209**

Principle 23: If you don't make time for health, you'd better make time for sickness   212

Principle 24: High performers take their MEDS   221

Principle 25: The future is utterly predictable   232

7: Take No Shortcuts   **239**

Principle 26: Success can be reverse-engineered   241

Principle 27: The best place to start is at the beginning   270

Reader's Guide   273

Acknowledgements   281

References   283

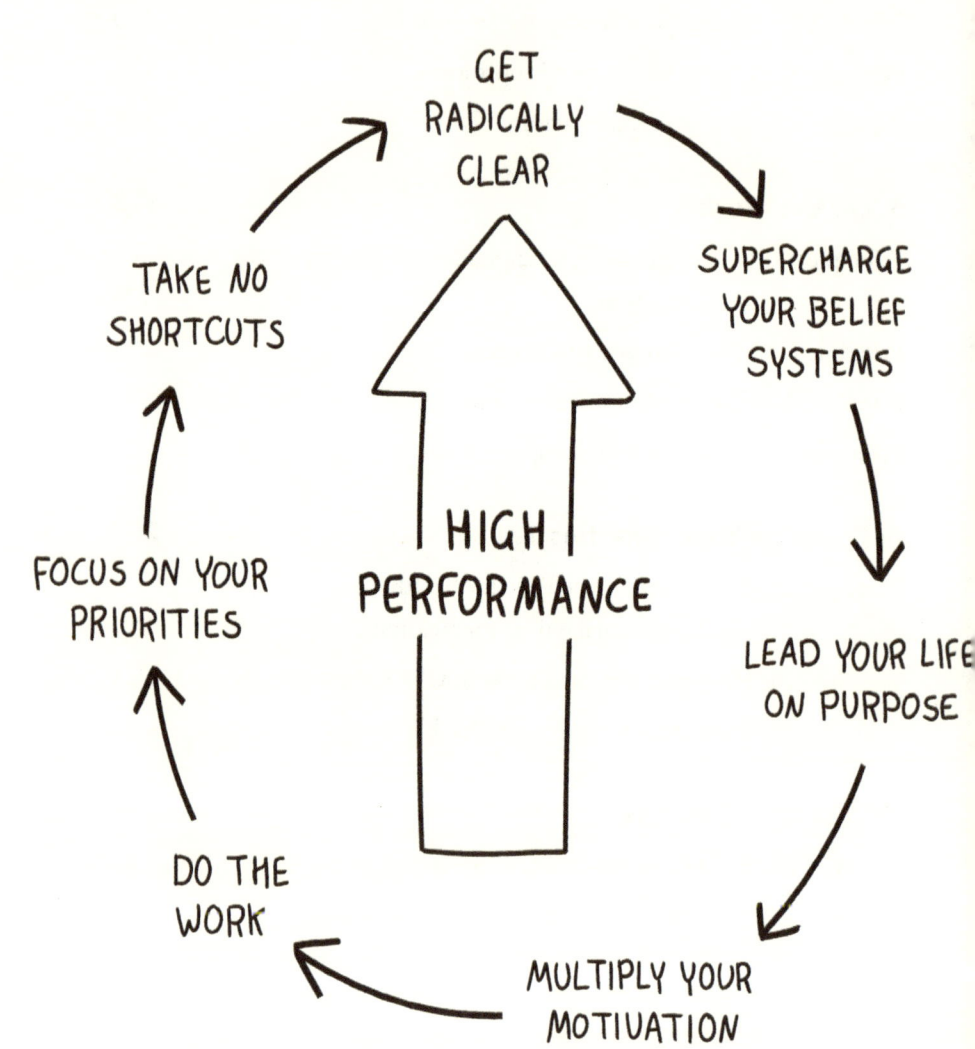

INTRODUCTION

A HIGH-PERFORMANCE LIFE IS YOURS FOR THE TAKING

Over the years I've had the good fortune of coaching, supporting, mentoring and interviewing some of the highest performers in sport, business and politics. And from thousands of hours of working with elite performers I've uncovered a simple set of truths about high performance. No matter who I've worked with, these same seven truths show up repeatedly.

In this book I will walk you through each of these seven key areas of high performance, and equip you with the tools you need to perform at the next level. Anyone can use these tools, whatever their industry or occupation. Many of them are informed by neuroscience, psychology and acclaimed research. High performers who've walked the walk and performed at the highest level in their respective arenas of life and business deeply reinforce them.

Over the past five years, I have amassed hundreds of hours of interviews with prime ministers, Formula One coaches, rare-air athletes, captains of world-champion teams, head coaches of those teams, world-renowned psychologists, *New York Times* bestselling authors and titans of the corporate world.

Not too long ago, these intimate insights were reserved for the elite few, but incredible advancements in technology have made this information globally accessible. I've released all of the interviews on my show, the *Habits of High Performers* podcast. It has been a joy to watch the show impact hundreds of thousands of people across the globe, with consistent top rankings on the Apple charts – including many number-one spots – around the world.

There are so many names for high performance – best-in-field, world-class, rare-air and peak performance, among others. Regardless of what you call it, connecting with it is what's truly important. The fact that you're reading this book is evidence that high performance is who you are and what you're destined for.

This book isn't a shortcut to success. It's not for someone who wants to be an overnight sensation. It's a book for the high performer who's willing to commit to a set of timeless truths. This collection of principles will be a game-changer for whoever commits to playing the long game.

A high-performance life is yours for the taking

Successful people are clear on where they're headed. They start with the end in mind and work backwards to reverse-engineer a high-performance life. Simply put, they do the work. They identify a small number of daily actions and perform them consistently over many years. Some onlookers might consider it boring. I once had the top performer of a global company sit on stage in front of his peers and take us through a day in his life. What he told us was unsurprising to me yet bewildering to many. He spoke of a structured day, a small number of critical commitments, and space created to nurture wellbeing and key relationships. There was nothing overly exciting, just simple things done well. High performers make a habit of doing the work. And they do the most important work first, before all else.

Habits of High Performers is all about doing what matters most, being clear on your outcomes, and committing to rituals that will move you closer to them. It's basic common sense, but common sense is rarely common practice. You won't find complex theories dotted throughout this book. Nor will you find many purely hopeful tactics. What you will uncover is a set of truths. I believe wholeheartedly in these truths, and I hope by the end you will too. The greats who I feature in the chapters ahead all embody these pragmatic principles in their purposeful lives.

Why does the world so often celebrate overnight sensations and people who get famous from a 30-second video, rather than those who consistently, and often quietly, build their brilliance over many years? Societal expectations are such that we feel obliged to be great at everything we do. Look polished in every photo. Be the perfect parent. Have an impeccable relationship. Don the finest designer wear. Even if people achieve these things by taking shortcuts, they seem to be applauded. But high performers approach life with a different understanding. They know that greatness lives in going deep. Deep with one thing. One passion. One skill. One hobby. One sport. One career. Whatever it might be, high performers know that it's imperative to focus on less. The world's greatest thought leaders, for example, are aware that it's better to talk a lot about a little than a little about a lot.

Simply put, high performance is about consistently exceeding norms while maintaining healthy relationships and wellbeing. Nothing more, nothing less. Achieving a gold medal once isn't high performance. Nor is achieving a plethora of wins while damaging your body or mind. Even consistently achieving epic results while maintaining your wellbeing but neglecting your key relationships doesn't fit the bill in my opinion.

Winning one game, having one great financial quarter is simply not enough. In sport it's often called a fluke. In the music industry you might be called a one-hit wonder. True high performers show their consistency by winning again and again. They dominate their field for decades, not days.

The second component of high performance requires you to commit to maintaining healthy relationships and your own wellbeing. I believe that success without fulfilment is not truly success. The richness of life is found in real relationships and thorough wellbeing. We spend much of our adult life working, but that should never be to the detriment of our personal relationships. Just remember that when you retire, the people who will still be there for you are your family and friends. High performers make time for the people who matter most to them. Being a better person outside of work makes you better at work. It's a package deal.

The secret to achieving this outcome is to embrace a specific set of 27 principles that I developed from thousands of hours spent with great leaders and performers, and from my own personal experiences as an entrepreneur and world-champion drummer. I've divided these principles into seven easily digestible chapters that reflect seven immutable truths of high performance.

It's not enough to do well in one or two of these key areas. To be truly successful, you must be committed to embracing all seven. Each complements the others. In fact, each relies on the others. They work in tandem to drive you towards best-in-field results.

I want you to consider each of the 27 principles as chunks of mini-mentoring that you can consume at your own pace, preferably a few each day. These come with high-performance rituals – exercises that will show you where you are and keep you on track towards your goals. The idea is to integrate the lessons and high-performance rituals so that, in time, they become habits.

Before you move on to Chapter 1, I highly recommend that you grab a blank journal to take notes, explore your thoughts and complete the high-performance rituals I prescribe throughout. This will help you to engage with the principles and exercises more fully and to keep track of your progress. I'll let you know as we go whenever you'll want to have your journal handy. I have created some powerful downloadable worksheets in a resource library available at www.jjlaughlin.com/habitbook, which is also available through the QR code provided below, and alongside each exercise throughout the book.

As you read, you are going to sit alongside some of the world's greatest leaders, performers and artists, and hear their stories. They include political figures, billionaires, professional athletes, business titans and thought leaders, such as:

- Samuel Whitelock – the most-capped New Zealand All Black rugby union star and world champion
- Dr Ellen Langer – the mother of mindfulness
- Scott O'Neil – CEO of LIV Golf, former CEO of Madison Square Garden and the Philadelphia 76ers US NBA team
- Sir John Key – former prime minister of New Zealand
- Anthony Trucks – US NFL star
- Marc Allen – co-founder of New World Library publishing company

- Michael Phelps – champion swimmer and the world's most decorated Olympian
- Duro Oye – former criminal mastermind turned philanthropist
- Alice Law – author of *Unstressable*
- Zion Armstrong – former Commonwealth Games athlete and former president of Adidas North America
- Aleix Casanovas – Formula One racing performance coach for George Russell
- Daniel Pink – best-selling author of *Drive*
- Dean Karnazes – ultramarathon runner and author of *Ultramarathon Man*
- Sir Steve Hansen – former head coach of the All Blacks rugby union side, the world's most dominant sports team
- Jason Redman – retired US Navy SEAL

Here is a breakdown of what you will learn in each chapter:

1. **Get Radically Clear**
   Vision precedes victory in every aspect of life and work. Without a vision, we can't get close to our potential. Radical clarity of vision will set you apart – it's the difference that *makes* the difference.
2. **Supercharge Your Belief Systems**
   You must believe it if you hope to achieve it. Your belief systems shape how you see the world around you, from your relationship with money to your ideas

about failure and power. Supercharging your beliefs is a surefire way to a high-performance life.

3. **Lead Your Life on Purpose**

   Life or work that lacks purpose isn't a life destined for high performance. Without a sense of purpose, high performance simply isn't sustainable over the long term. This chapter will help you uncover why you do what you do, and help you supercharge your life with a sense of purpose.

4. **Multiply Your Motivation**

   Extrinsic and intrinsic motivation are important factors in helping us move towards a goal. The high performers we all look up to know how to tap into the right one at the right time.

5. **Do the Work**

   The difference between winning and losing is discipline. Talent isn't the defining factor of high-performing people. Consistent action beats lazy talent every day of the week.

6. **Focus on Your Priorities**

   Success in sport or business without the riches of healthy relationships and wellbeing isn't high performance. This chapter is all about being a high performer with a holistic approach.

7. **Take No Shortcuts**

   People who dream without a plan are dreamers. A dream *with* a plan is a recipe for progress. To fulfil your ambitions, you will need plans, goals and priorities. High performers are elite action-takers.

A high-performance life is yours for the taking

Instant gratification isn't part of a high-performance life. If high performance is your desired outcome, then it's essential to draw up a plan that takes no shortcuts.

Working through this chapter will ensure you have a roadmap for success. If you're serious about high performance in life and work, then you will need a system. *This* is your system.

So let's dive in and begin your high-performance journey by getting radically clear.

1
GET RADICALLY CLEAR

Here's a timeless truth: *Vision precedes victory.* When you peel back the layers of a high-performing athlete, entrepreneur or leader, you will always find that they have a radically clear vision. Radical clarity is what separates great from greatest. Knowing exactly where you're headed, with zero doubts, is a level of clarity that will allow you to move forward with ease. When you're radically clear, you're so passionate about your goal that saying no to distractions is second nature. People who lack radical clarity tend not to have priorities and are prone to procrastination.

High performers simply know exactly where they're headed. They can see the endpoint, feel it, hear it and even taste it. They connect deeply with the victory they chase. And yet most will admit that they didn't know exactly how they would get there. That's where most of us get stuck. We get caught up in the detail, the step-by-step minutiae, which leaves us feeling overwhelmed and unable to move forward.

The all-time greats I've worked with, coached, interviewed and learned from all share one common theme: a crystal-clear vision of what success looks like – *to them*. And that personal nature of their vision is the crucial point here. Too many people create a life vision that's deeply influenced and shaped by society, or their parents, teachers or social circles. Have you sometimes made significant decisions based on what you thought others would think about you? Perhaps it was a university degree you took, a career path you pursued, a car you bought or even the clothes you wear. When leaders and high performers start to play in the rare air of greatness, they shed the weight of societal expectations, embrace their unique passion and purpose, and march to the beat of their own drum.

One of the most revered sports teams on the planet is New Zealand's professional rugby union team, the All Blacks. They are the most successful international men's rugby side of all time, with a winning percentage of 76.77 per cent across hundreds of tests. For global corporate organisations, as well as professional sports teams, the All Blacks are often considered a prime example of what greatness looks like. Their culture is admired around the globe and they have backed it up with multiple world rugby titles. Over the years I've had the pleasure of interacting with the All Blacks in various ways: some players have taken part in my leadership mastermind programmes, I've helped a number of them with the mental side of their game, I've interviewed their head coaches, and I've developed long-lasting friendships with a handful of them.

Each and every one of these players and coaches had a radically clear vision of what success looked like to them, but one player really stuck out to me: Samuel Whitelock. Sam's commitment to consistently pursuing his vision is second to none, and he carries himself with humility.

Being in the company of a high performer who knows what they're about while remaining true to their values is something special. All too often, people get so caught up in their status, results and performance that they forget what's most important and quickly become arrogant.

This great All Black is one of four brothers who have represented their country at international level, and part of a family in which several generations have also played professional sport. Sam is a great human, on and off the field. On the field, he was known for going the extra mile. He would be the first to arrive and the last to leave. He would push his body to its limits and he consistently put his team before his own needs. Outside the arena, it was clear to me that family is what matters most to him. He prioritises time spent with his wife and kids. He also makes a huge effort to make a difference in the community by giving up his time for charitable work.

A mutual friend introduced us several years ago, and he joined one of my mastermind coaching programmes sometime later. He brought great humility to the table, along with a significant appetite for learning and growing. At this point, he had played professional sport for the majority of his adult life, had been part of the Rugby World Cup–winning team twice and had captained the team 18 times. He had played alongside the greatest players the rugby world has ever seen, yet he remained humble and deeply rooted in family values – most notably respect, connection and integrity. He would always be the one to challenge other leaders in the group as to why they were doing certain things, where they were headed and what their end game was. Several months into the programme he shared something with the group that highlighted his uniqueness – his personal vision. It was July 2021, and Samuel had 123 caps for the All Blacks. He told us that he wanted to be the most capped All Black of all time, so he needed to reach 149 caps. He wanted to stay in the game long enough to achieve this goal, while continuing to bring massive value to the team by performing at the elite level. This was a radically clear vision if ever I heard one.

In essence, Sam was sharing with my mastermind coaching group his commitment to playing the long game. If high performance is your goal, the long game is the only game worth playing. Playing the long game is not something everybody is willing to do, because it's tough, uncertain and requires a great deal of sacrifice. Factors that were out of Samuel's control could have impacted his audacious goal, such as games being postponed due to Covid, or him being injured or not selected. Nevertheless, he was able to articulate what it would feel like to achieve his goal, what it would look like and why it was so important to him.

Get Radically Clear

To put Sam's goal in perspective, more than 1200 people have played for the All Blacks since the team's first Test match in 1903, yet only 12 of those had managed to pull on the black jersey 100 times or more. Many players only stepped onto the field a handful of times, some only once or twice, before being dropped from the squad. True high performance is about performing at the elite level with longevity – sustaining success over the long term. Many of the greats in sport talk about having set their personal vision as being the greatest of all time in their chosen field. If you want to be a high performer, the long game is the only game to play.

Fast forward to 2023 and the end was nigh for Whitelock's international career. New Zealand Rugby had confirmed that he would be playing his final campaign as an All Black at the Rugby World Cup in France. His clarity of vision, unwavering self-belief and relentless work ethic ensured that he was selected. After New Zealand's first two matches, Sam had drawn level with the then most-capped All Black player, Richie McCaw, at 148 caps.

I'll never forget watching Sam take the field against Italy in New Zealand's third match of the World Cup knockouts and become the most capped All Black of all time. It reinforced on so many levels that setting an inspiring, almost daunting, vision for yourself and sharing it with your inner circle is integral to bringing that vision to life. Samuel Whitelock finished his career on 153 caps, and the message from Richie McCaw says it all: 'A massive congrats to Samuel on becoming the most capped All Black. It takes huge amounts of drive and perseverance along with a relentless consistency to play as many games as you have.'

Becoming radically clear is the essential starting point for high-performance results. When you're radically clear, you're not distracted by shiny objects. You're not unsure about your next steps. You're not asking everybody for their thoughts on your decisions. When you're radically clear, you're highly focused on what's most important. Nothing will throw you off course. You are decisive and sure about your next steps. You don't need reassurance or approval from others about your decisions and goals.

By the end of this chapter, you will be radically clear. To get there, our first five principles will be your stepping stones:

1. Always play the long game.
2. Make time for what's most important (WMI).
3. Values make the vision.
4. Diluting your priorities will dilute your results.
5. Get out of your head and onto the page.

Principle 1: Always play the long game

Why do some embrace a long-game vision while others settle for the short game? Because we, as humans, get stuck. It's easy to find yourself in a loop of indecision. Quick wins and short-term goals are often more appealing. The thought of delayed gratification isn't exactly tantalising. In this fast-paced world, we're wired to achieve more in less time. We're hooked on getting results instantly and effortlessly.

Ambition, belief, awareness, drive, life experiences and fear are the key drivers that shape how an individual sets their vision, either for themselves or their organisation. The short game can be anything from six months to several years. Humans tend to overestimate what they can achieve in a year and underestimate what they can achieve in a decade. Short-game thinking is safe, tangible and reasonable. Society often labels long-game thinkers as crazy, unrealistic and sometimes even unsafe.

On a number of occasions, I've invited my friend Sir John Key, former prime minister of New Zealand, onto my podcast to share his story. To me, his approach to life has been of the long-game variety. It is obvious he had a radically clear vision from a very young age. Around eight or nine, he explicitly told his mother that he intended to make a million dollars and then become the prime minister. Now that's a powerful demonstration of setting specific and ambitious goals.

John's mother left her home country of Austria as a 16-year-old Jewish refugee, having escaped as the Nazis invaded. She eventually ended up in New Zealand with her husband. When he passed away from a heart attack shortly after, she was left to raise three children. John told me, 'I was really raised by my mum and I have no memory at all of Dad. Mum was a very determined woman and told me that you've got to focus on the thing that they can never take away from you, which is education. She also instilled the belief that in the end, you get out of life what you put into it.' It seems obvious that John's mum was teaching her children the long-game way of thinking from when they were very young.

John graduated from the University of Canterbury in Christchurch in 1981 with a Bachelor of Commerce degree. His commitment to his initial goal of becoming a millionaire took him on a career path with Merrill Lynch, where he became the global head of foreign exchange. His time with the company led to his appointment as a member of the Foreign Exchange Committee of the Federal Reserve Bank of New York from 1999 to 2001. He didn't win the lottery or get rich quick; he played the long game. He showed up and did the work consistently over the long term. This long-game approach was clearly part of his plan for success.

Having achieved the first of his two dream goals, in the early 2000s he returned to New Zealand to join one of the nation's major political parties. This party suffered a significant defeat in the 2002 election, but John stayed the course, eventually becoming the party leader in 2006.

On 19 November 2008, John Key was sworn in as New Zealand's prime minister. Sadly his mum didn't live to witness him achieving the goal he'd shared with her several decades earlier. John led the party to two more general election wins, and along the way navigated the 2007–2008 Global Financial Crisis and the 2010–2011 Christchurch earthquakes.

Sir John Key is a fine example of an ordinary guy who achieved extraordinary things. By having a radically clear vision and a willingness to patiently play the long game, he was able to bring his two dream goals to fruition.

Playing the long game requires single-mindedness, hard work and commitment, both of which are evident in John's illustrious career. Just showing up year after year won't help you create a high-performance life. What truly matters is your attitude and work ethic. Whatever your vision looks like, be sure to apply consistent effort and commit to the long game.

Most of us could look at what Sir John did to achieve success and agree that it was largely common sense. But common sense is rarely common practice.

Make sure your long game is *your* game

If you want to play it small and safe, opt for the short game. But if you want to be a high performer, then play the long game. The key risk of playing small is regret. Do you want to get to the end of your life, this one shot you've been given, and feel a deep sense of regret that you didn't act on your dreams? My bet is you'll have more regret about the things you didn't do than the things you did.

Do you know the number one regret people have when they die? They say, 'I wish I'd had the courage to live a life true to myself, not the life others expected of me.' Bronnie Ware, a palliative care nurse, spent years working with patients who were in the last days and weeks of their lives. She asked each of them what they regretted about the lives they'd lived and how they might do it differently if they had another shot. The overwhelming regret was that they lived their lives making choices based on what they thought others wanted them to do or be. How sad, yet how common.

So many people have come up to me after I've given a presentation and said to me, 'I hate my job, but I just don't think I can switch careers. It's who I am, it's my identity.' They're playing the short game. They just can't see any other possibilities in their current reality. But when I challenge them to take a longer-term view – over ten to twenty years, say – they start to see the clouds lift. Too many people think no further than a one-year period. This can make the idea of achieving your goals daunting – after all, good things take time. When you're setting a vision, it's critical that you allow yourself more space and time so that you can step into it with confidence. You need to know you have a long enough runway for your dreams to fly into reality.

The best lessons in life come from experience and failure. They go hand in hand and require you to push yourself, get outside your comfort zone and try new things. A meaningful life isn't created by sitting on your sofa watching Netflix three hours a day. A life of purpose begins when you step outside your house and into the world.

The long-term consequence of being a short-game thinker is regret. But most people find it easy to turn a blind eye to the long-term pain their everyday habits will cause. Take food, for example. Many people are happy to eat ultra-processed fast food because it suits their time-poor life, but they don't spend much time (if any) thinking about the cumulative impact of this habit on their internal organs over the long run. The one-percenters who dominate their industries and take charge of their lives can skip forward in their mind to experience what life will look like in 20, 30 or even 50 years. They can generate the feelings and paint the pictures of how their life will be if they continue to make conscious daily choices, habits and behaviours.

When you develop a clear enough vision of yourself and your future, anything is possible. As you work through this book, you'll do lots of exercises that will help you refine your long-term vision and develop the day-to-day tools you need to make it a reality. Your micro-habits dictate your macro life.

Principle 2: Make time for what's most important (WMI)

The pace of modern society often forces us to focus on the wrong WMI. How often do you give your attention to what's most imminent rather than what's most important? Usually we're distracted by the thing that's right in front of us. Maybe it's a text that just came through. Maybe it's a colleague with an urgent request. Maybe it's a social media notification. But if we want high performance to be within our reach, we need to take a different approach to WMI. High performers consistently take action towards what's most important.

I often meet people who seemingly have it all but are less than fulfilled inside. You know the people I'm talking about. They have the great careers, the nice cars, the big holidays, the perfect family life. From their Instagram highlight reels or LinkedIn posts they seem like high performers. But behind closed doors they're living lives devoid of meaning and fulfilment. And success without fulfilment is ultimately failure.

I had a friend on my podcast who used to fit this description. He was a linebacker for the Pittsburgh Steelers in the US National Football League (NFL), and an *American Ninja Warrior* star on NBC. From afar, Anthony Trucks looked like a high performer, but the odds were stacked against him from the outset. In fact, he probably should never have reached those glorious heights of success.

When he was three years old, his mum took him and his three siblings and put them into the American foster-care system. He told me that in the United States, 'statistically, 75 per cent of prison inmates are former foster kids; 50 per cent of the homeless population have spent time in foster care and less than 1 per cent of foster kids graduate from college'.

Foster care damaged him and his siblings. As a six-year-old African American, he ended up in a white family where he struggled to navigate his identity, not really knowing where he fit in. At 14 he was finally adopted and his life began. Sadly, his foster mum was then diagnosed with MS and his older brother headed off to the military.

He almost gave up on life at a very young age and was on track to becoming a statistic. He lost hope for the future and was in a dark place mentally. But instead of giving up, he set his sights on something different. He decided he'd beat the odds by becoming great and doing something amazing. He worked incredibly hard towards something that didn't make sense in the moment, but he formulated a plan that he then executed, and won a football scholarship to the University of Oregon. He then went on to play in the NFL. As a young athlete, he married and had kids.

At this point in his life, an onlooker would likely have defined Anthony as a high performer. He had it all. Until a fluke shoulder injury sent his NFL dreams crashing down just as quickly as they'd come.

'I then broke my life and my marriage fell apart,' he says. 'The business I started was almost bankrupt, I wasn't a present father and had twins on the way. I didn't like myself post-football and it got to the point where I genuinely wanted to take my own life. I thought, "If this is life post-football, I don't want to be here."'

You might ask how on earth he got to this point. He'd successfully navigated a lot of the ambushes that life sent his way. But he was forced to navigate many different challenges simultaneously. And when we focus on the imminent many over the critical few, the wheels start to fall off. Where your focus goes, your energy flows.

It's obvious that Anthony had forgotten to focus on what's most important. His life was chaotic, almost to the point of no return. How did he navigate going past being a foster kid? Navigate past losing his football identity? Navigate past losing his mum? Navigate past losing his marriage? How did the business keep going?

That's where Anthony realised it was an identity thing. He got clear on WMI and made shifts to course-correct his life each time an ambush struck. Shaping his identity was the most important thing for him. 'I realised that the answer for me was to see, shift, sustain,' he shared. 'I see what's gotta be done, I craft a plan. I shift, I do the work and execute consistently. Sustain. I commit to it over time.' For him, it was all about staying focused on curating the identity that would help him perform at his best. It began with awareness and being able to see the issue and the potential way forward. Followed by making the shift and then of course playing the long game to integrate his new identity.

Anthony has kept WMI at the heart of everything he does. He did get divorced, but then he repaired the marriage and has become a present father. He now runs an amazing business and is a sought-after international speaker.

High performance is more than your career

Failing is succeeding, but only when we take what we learn from our failures and apply it to our lives. A business owner approached me in recent years and asked if I would be his coach. He was running an organisation that was growing rapidly and he wanted to see how far he could take it in terms of revenue, impact and team size. He was willing to win at all costs on the career front. But when I gave him a short self-assessment so he could get a fix on the key pillars of his life and help him define where he was at with WMI, he was shocked by what he saw on the page. It was clear that his intimate relationship didn't feature in his priorities, and that his commitment to his physical health was practically non-existent. Yet he was committed to striving for a high performance life. He quickly realised that winning on the field (in his case in his career) was only going to bring him fulfilment and meaning if he was also winning off the field (in everything other than his career). This realisation might seem like common sense, but as I've said already, common sense isn't always common practice.

Before you move on to setting your vision, make sure you get clear on what's most important. Some examples of what's most important are: the warm greeting you share with your loved one when you return home rather than taking that after-hours work call as you arrive home. A lunchtime gym session rather than eating your sandwich while sitting at your desk and powering through some emails. Being fully present on your holiday rather than checking your work emails throughout the day.

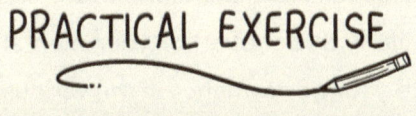 

THE SEVEN PILLARS OF WMI

To get clear on where you're at with your personal WMI, you need to have a handle on the seven pillars of WMI:

1. Heartset
2. Health
3. Personal growth
4. Relationships
5. Wealth
6. Joy
7. Career

As you work towards becoming a high performer, I want you to commit to a monthly WMI check-in for each of these areas. Schedule a five-minute meeting with yourself. Make it a repeating event on your calendar for the last day of each month. I'm not kidding. Take out your phone now and add a recurring monthly event. Once you get to Chapter 7, you will also use this time to check-in on your priorities for the month ahead.

Step 1: Prepare yourself

Take out your journal (if you don't have one, get one now) and write out the seven pillars of WMI, one to a page.

Each of these pillars is an area of your life that needs ongoing attention and focus. Neglecting any of them for too long is guaranteed to create stress and chaos. Getting radically clear on your personal WMI will lead to a more fulfilling and meaningful life with benefits for your mental and physical wellbeing and your performance in the various domains of your life.

Step 2: Score yourself

The check-in involves considering the past month of your life and assigning yourself a score anywhere between −15 and +15 for each pillar. In this scoring system, −15 would represent an absence of high performance in that pillar, 0 neutrality or mediocrity, and +15 no room for improvement. Each time you do your monthly WMI check-in, stay clear on what each pillar encompasses and how you might score it:

Get Radically Clear

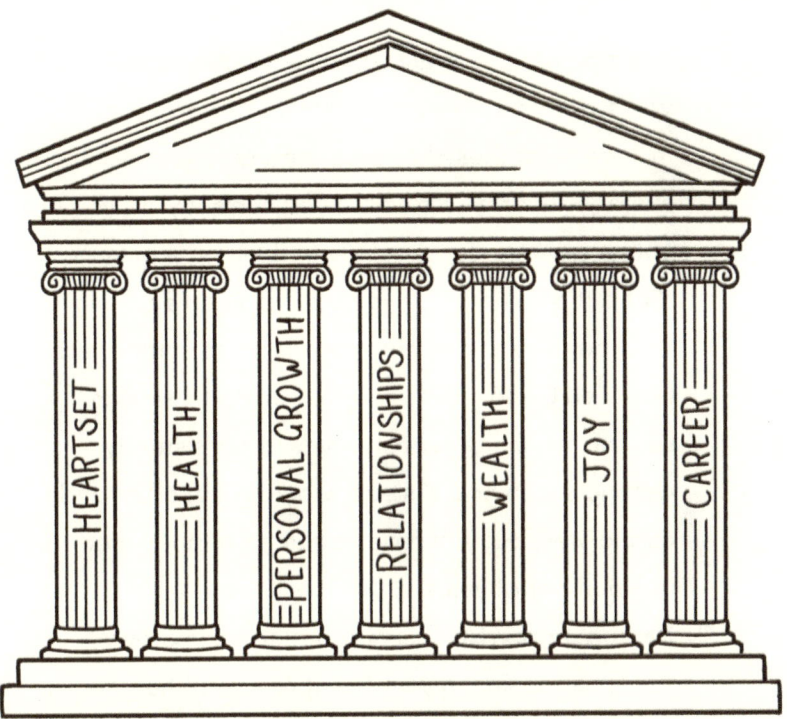

1. **Heartset**: This pillar relates to your emotional and mental wellbeing. More specifically, it assesses how you're responding to challenges and stressors at work and at home. If you're experiencing high highs and low lows, then you might sit somewhere around −10 to −15. If you're more mellow and neutral and struggle to tap into your emotions, then perhaps you're closer to the 0 mark. And if you feel deeply connected to your emotional awareness and can manage it effectively, then perhaps you might sit around the +10 to +15.
2. **Health**: This pillar is all-encompassing, including your physical health, strength, stamina, sleep,

nutrition and general overall health metrics. As you score yourself in this pillar it's important to include all of these key areas and give yourself an average that reflects where you currently sit. If you're working out regularly and eating a balanced diet but getting only five hours of sleep each night, then perhaps you might score yourself somewhere between 0 and −5. You'd give yourself a similar score if, on the other hand, you're consistently getting seven hours' sleep, working out often and eating well, but you haven't had a full-body medical in a number of years.

3. **Personal growth**: This pillar reflects the growth that's happening in your life. It relates to heightening your self-awareness and improving your emotional quotient (EQ), and also how much you're growing your skills through reading, listening and/or studying. When scoring yourself here, perhaps ask yourself how much time you've spent reading this month. Or how many hours you've listened to informative podcasts on your topic of choice. Or perhaps your learning is more formal, and so you can rank yourself on your progress with a degree or certificate.

4. **Relationships**: This pillar relates to the state of your closest relationships, including friends, family and your intimate partner, if you have one. When assessing yourself in this area, it's important to ask if your key connections are in a good place or

if they require work. Perhaps your social life is in high gear but you haven't spent any time with your family in a week or three. In that case, perhaps you're a 0 to –5. Give yourself a similar score if, say, you've spent all your time with your intimate partner and neglected the rest of your family and friends. This exercise is designed to get you to think more openly about the important relationships in your life.

5. **Wealth**: You get to decide how to quantify this pillar. For some, it could be assessing your overall wealth position for long-term retirement. For others, it might be looking at your current cash-flow position. Maybe it's a combination of the two. However you think about wealth, please don't skim over this section. Financial pressure and mismanagement have serious consequences for our lives.

6. **Joy:** This pillar relates to how much time you're putting aside for fun and recreation. Success without joy is ultimately failure. When assessing your current position regarding this pillar, I want you to ask yourself how many activities you've engaged in during the past month that have filled your cup. They shouldn't be work-related. If you've only managed an hour or two of time for hobbies and fun, then perhaps you'd score yourself a –10. Or if you have one night a week to spend on a hobby,

and a few hours on the weekend for running in the hills, you might score yourself a +11.

7. **Career**: This pillar pertains to how you've felt about your career over the past month. Are you feeling valued and recognised? Perhaps that would score a +9. Or are you feeling burnt out, in which case you might be sitting at a −12. Take a moment to get clear on how this last month has been and how you're feeling about it all.

Step 3: Examine your scores

How do your scores look? In my experience, high performers or potential high performers often have high expectations and hold themselves to very high standards. This means that not scoring +15 in all seven pillars of WMI, all the time, can be triggering for some. But remember, this exercise is not about sitting at the upper end of every area of your life.

The point of the exercise is to truthfully identify how you feel about each pillar, and become more aware of which areas are your highest priority for the next month. In other words, you're more accurately identifying what's most important to you.

Each month, commit to spending more time nurturing your two lowest-scoring pillars. High performers know that complexity kills execution, so avoid writing down multiple actions for improving these pillars. Instead, simply write in your journal one simple thing you could work on for each pillar over the next month. Simplicity shapes success.

To help you with this exercise, here are some examples of a simple step you could commit to for each pillar – although of course you only want to focus on two at a time:

1. **Heartset**: Say you scored yourself a +4 because this past month has dealt you a handful of challenges and you're feeling anxious throughout the day. One simple action could be to commit to breathwork at lunchtime each day.
2. **Health**: If you scored yourself a –1 because in the past month you've been eating takeaway three nights a week on average, you could focus on weekly meal prep as your action step to improve in this area.
3. **Personal growth**: Maybe you've been looking at those books on your bedside table for weeks but haven't quite got around to reading them. Maybe you'd score yourself a 0? So your action step here could be to read three pages each night before falling asleep – chances are you'll end up reading way more than three pages once you get started.
4. **Personal relationships**: Perhaps you've scored yourself a +7 because you've been spending a lot of time connecting with friends yet only a small amount with your partner. Your one action step could be to schedule one date night a week for the next month.

5. **Wealth**: Say you gave yourself a −12 because you've splashed out on a new car when you really should have saved a little longer. Your one action step could be to create a spending plan for each week and actually stick to it.
6. **Joy**: Perhaps you scored yourself a 0 because you're fully focused on your career but not finding any time for adventure. You could spice things up a bit by locking in an activity that you've never tried before and doing that each week for a month.
7. **Career**: Imagine you scored yourself +11 in the career pillar because everything is ticking along nicely, yet you know there's more potential for growth. Perhaps your one action step could be to get curious and identify where that growth lies within your work.

These are all just suggestions, and I encourage you to explore what *better* looks like for you in each pillar. Remember, this is not about achieving +15 in every pillar. Striving for such a pointless goal will only create a lot of self-imposed pressure. Rather, it's about being aware of your life priorities.

You've now embraced a high-performance ritual that will help you become radically clear. Remember, if you don't make time for what's most important, you're making time for what's most imminent. Don't let other people's requests and problems become your to-do's. To get radically clear, you need to operate from a place of awareness.

Principle 3: Values make the vision

High performers are often described by their closest supporters as 'obsessed'. They relentlessly pursue better and they strive for growth. When you look under the hood of a high performer, you'll see something that drives that commitment and drowns out the noise. And that something is a set of core values.

Values are your personal guiding principles that shape how you make decisions. Knowing what you value will help you create a vision that's deeply aligned with your internal compass. Why is identifying your values important? Well, if your values align with the action you're taking, you will experience a deeper sense of meaning. The opposite is also true.

Five years ago, a CEO–founder who I was coaching asked me why he wasn't getting as much fulfilment or purpose from his life as he would have liked. It became clear that he valued family – in fact, it was his number-one core value and priority. Yet when I asked him to get his phone out to show me his calendar and credit card spending over the past month, things began to paint a different picture. Where we spend our time and money says a lot about our values. On average, this guy was devoting less than 4 per cent of his time to his loved ones, yet he was telling himself that family was his core value. By looking at the amount of time he was spending on various areas of his life each day – including sleep, work, gym, socialising, family time, eating and several other activities – we calculated that on most days, he was spending only 45–60 minutes with his family.

Trust me, this is a normal statistic among leaders across multiple industries. Please note that I said 'leaders' here, not 'high-performing leaders'. Because, as we know, high-performing leaders ensure they maintain healthy relationships and wellbeing while performing at the top of their field.

My client agreed to sit down a few weeks later to do the work – on himself. The first thing we did was identify his values and priorities, then we looked at how he could live his life in such a way as to reflect those values. A year later we reconnected and took another look at his life. It would be fair to say that his seven pillars of WMI, and his calendar activities, were looking much different. He'd almost doubled the average time he spent with his family, and had also seen a notable improvement in his physical fitness and business performance. This slight shift resulted in him feeling more fulfilled and connected with what was most important in his life.

The first step for him was to get radically clear on his values, followed by a time audit to see where he was *actually* spending his time. Once he started to adjust what he focused his time and attention on, he started authentically living by his values. This has served him well in recent years. He is making progress towards his long-game goals by letting his values make the vision. His wife and kids have commented that he's a more present and patient person. His body is measurably stronger and fitter than it was half a decade ago. And he has continued to move towards his ultimate goal of selling his company for a life-changing sum.

Our core values must reflect our long-term vision

Want to bring your vision to life as a high performer? The crucial step is to get your values locked and loaded. Here's an example what *not* to do. I was once invited into a large corporate organisation to help equip its executive leadership team with the skills required to build an enduring great company. The first question I asked the CEO was, 'What are your company values?' He proceeded to open his drawer and riffle through it to find a piece of paper. He then rattled off, 'Excellence, Integrity, Faith, Innovation, Persistence, Community …' I raised my hand and asked him how many values the company had. He said 11, to which I responded, 'You need 11 values to run this company? I don't know a lot about the Bible but I'm pretty confident that Moses only needed ten for the entire world.' I received a belly laugh in response from the leader and many of his team. We all agreed that the majority of the workforce wouldn't be able to remember most of those values and therefore they could never be truly lived.

A few meaningful values will help guide your life in a direction you will be proud of. It needs to be only a few because research shows that our working memory capacity is limited. Our brains can only handle small chunks of information at a time – typically just three to five pieces. No matter how much we try to group or rehearse things, we're limited by this capacity. When we're solving problems, planning or trying to understand something complex, it's essential that we focus on breaking things down into manageable pieces.

To avoid overload and achieve high performance, we need to simplify things and work with smaller, digestible chunks of information.

Take the time now, by engaging in the ritual below, to get clear on your three core values so that you can allow them to inform the decisions you make in pursuit of your vision. Radically clear values will move you towards a radically clear vision.

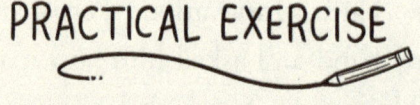 

PRACTICAL EXERCISE

CORE VALUES SELF-ASSESSMENT

Once again, grab your journal. It's time to get clear on your core values – those personal ideals that will help you make decisions with radical clarity. Having clear values will also help you nurture your relationships and achieve your goals.

Step 1: Identify the traits you admire in others

Write the heading 'What I value in other people is …' and beneath it identify all of the traits you value in others. For example, loyalty, honesty, integrity, commitment and so on. Take your time to write as much as you can. If you're struggling, think about your closest friends or family members and identify what you love most about them.

Next, write the heading 'When I'm not within earshot, what I'd like others to say they value about me is …' Beneath that, note all of the traits that come to mind. It might, for example, be kindness, perseverance, empathy or forgiveness. Take the time to really think this through, and be sure to look at it from a personal and professional point of view. Include any values that come to mind.

Now comes the difficult part, narrowing it down to just three core values. Circle the values from both lists to which you feel the strongest connection. The ones you haven't circled still matter a lot to you, but they're not your *core* values. Getting to the most important three values will allow you more freedom to make decisions effectively and efficiently.

This first step might take a few sittings, or you might nail it in one go. Write your final three values on a fresh page in your journal.

Step 2: Create a mantra for living each value
Knowing your values and living them are two different things. Many people are able to rattle off their values, yet few are able to define how they bring their values to life. High performers embody their values. Here I want you to formulate a command. Beside each of your three core values, write down a command that will help you stay the course and make your values a way of being, not just words on a page. Each one should be a clear call to action.

Here are some examples of the sorts of things I mean.

Value	Command
Intuition	Trust your gut
Honesty	Do the right thing
Empathy	Seek to understand

Value	Command
Discipline	Do the work
Perseverance	Keep moving forward
Courage	Take bold action
Gratitude	Acknowledge the good
Authenticity	Be real
Humility	Stay grounded

As you can see, the commands are incredibly simple, and each has four words or less. Later we will discuss our working memory's inability to hold more than three to five chunks of information at a time, but for now let's use that knowledge to our advantage and give ourselves a high-performance edge.

Doing your values

High performers know that values make the vision. They know the hidden secret that most other people don't: how to actually *do* your values. I've met so many people, and teams, who have values up on a wall or on their website … yet they can't clearly articulate how to *do* those values.

Think of Nike for a moment, arguably one of the greatest shoe brands of all time. What do you think their number one core value might be? Well, look at their brand mantra: *Just do it*. It's a call to action, a command. I feel that their core value is execution, as in 'less talk and more action'. Walk the walk, don't just talk the talk. The 'Just do it' mantra ripples right across the organisation at all levels, inspiring team members to execute their mission of bringing inspiration and innovation to every athlete in the world. Simplicity is the starting point for success. Keep it simple and act. When we start to make processes complex, or have a long to-do list, it's enough to stall us. And suddenly we're caught in a loop of procrastination and the torment of overthinking. Never forget that complexity kills progress.

You are a human, not a robot. Your values are a guiding principle, a compass of sorts. When you start to stray or wobble, they will help you get back on track towards your radically clear vision.

Through my leadership work and my podcast, I have the privilege of access to some of the world's most notable decision-makers, including several heads of state and government leaders.

I recently sat down with David Seymour, co-deputy prime minister of New Zealand. Unlike a political commentator, I prefer to spend less time talking about controversy and more time talking about character. When I have a leader in front of me, no matter where they sit on the political spectrum, my one and only goal is to get them out of their head and into their heart. This is where they open up and share their real self.

The first time I sat down with David, we talked about a wide array of topics. What I really wanted to know, though, was how he made decisions and what values kept him true to his word. I was shocked and delighted when he pulled out his wallet and read a little note aloud. He'd created it many years earlier at a personal growth seminar and it had been tucked in his wallet ever since. It reminded him of what brings purpose and meaning to his life's vision.

Here's what David identified as his guiding values, the core principles that help him to hold himself accountable to a life well-lived:

1. Speak well of others.
2. Seek and recognise the best in each person.
3. Use my time on earth to leave the planet and people better than I found it.
4. Be self-aware and take responsibility for my actions.
5. Be kind to myself today.
6. Make decisions that are kind to my future.

What's the point in having these core principles? We come to many crossroads in life. Without core principles, we can find ourselves making decisions flippantly or thoughtlessly. But when we have a set of guiding values, we can check whether our decision is true to our values before we commit to it.

David was upfront and admitted that he doesn't live up to his ideals every single day. In that moment, my appreciation of him grew – he showed honesty, humility and a deep sense of humanity. We all need guiding principles if we want to achieve high-performance outcomes and look back on our life with pride and self-respect.

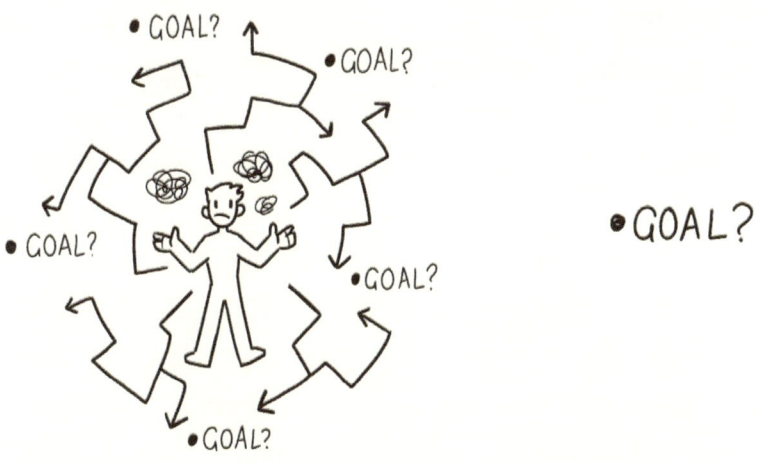

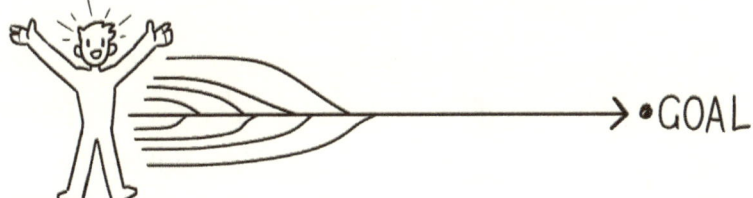

Principle 4: Diluting your priorities will dilute your results

John runs a large investment firm. A number of years ago he was experiencing some challenges in his business and in his personal life. On field he wasn't hitting the revenue numbers he knew his business could achieve, and off field he was having problems in his marriage. 'I'm just so busy, James,' he said. 'That's why I'm not getting the results I know I could get. That's also the reason why I'm not present with my partner – I simply don't have the time.' I'd heard it all before from business owners, athletes and everyday people. Time and time again, I know they are simply deluding themselves.

My response was this. 'John, let's get your iPhone out and look at your screen time over the past few weeks.' He was hesitant and a little frustrated with me, although he humoured me. What did we discover? Well, his most used app was Instagram, at a whopping average of nine hours every week. The next two most used apps were also social media platforms. 'John, you spend more than a working day each week on Instagram. How many clients have you got via Insta, how much revenue has that brought in, and how many do you communicate with through that channel?'

The silence was deafening. He sheepishly piped up, 'Zero.'

We quickly concluded that he didn't have a time problem, he had a priority problem. Later in the book you will learn how to rewire your brain using neuroscience-backed techniques, but for now let's get clear that your priorities will dictate your outcomes. Plain and simple. High-performing people focus on their priorities. They are the one-percenters who double down on what's most important and guard their mind like it's a fortress. Jim Collins, the great author and management consultant, said in *Good to Great* that the truly great leaders consistently focus on the 'critical few over the important many'.

Focus on your critical few priorities

We each sit on the priority spectrum somewhere between those who have large to-do lists and jump at every opportunity presented ... and those who radically focus on a critical few priorities while saying no to anything outside of those. I wanted to investigate this issue further, so I invited Greg McKeown, the author of the bestselling book *Essentialism*, onto my podcast. He confirmed, through deep research, that those who sit on the first side of the spectrum are non-essentialists.

'They are on an undisciplined pursuit of more,' Greg explained. They tend to take on too many tasks, commitments and responsibilities without careful consideration of what's most important. He added, 'They are driven by a belief that they can have it all and do it all, and often end up accomplishing less and feeling unsatisfied because their efforts are scattered.'

The opposite type of person is the essentialist, someone who is on a disciplined pursuit of less. As Greg explained, 'They make deliberate choices, prioritising what matters most and saying no to the many other distractions.' Essentialists live by design, not default. High performers must embrace the essentialist life.

Which end of the spectrum do you sit on? Are you diluting your priorities and consequently diluting your results?

Many humans focus on the 'important many' each and every day. They have to-do lists, they have lots of social engagements, they keep up with all of the Netflix series, they say yes to almost everything, they are often trying to please others. But high achievers remain focused on the 'critical few'. They identify their priorities and they stick to them like glue. They say no to distractions, they do the work to improve themselves, they are happy to enforce boundaries, and they feed their minds with books and courses. They are able to successfully balance their life, work and relationships.

When you have ten priorities you have a to-do list. You will simply join the masses and get busy being busy. But when you play the long game, you agree to getting radically clear on your priorities and stepping into each and every day with full focus on the few things that are most important.

PRACTICAL EXERCISE

IDENTIFY YOUR TOP FIVE PRIORITIES

Whip out your journal and identify your top five priorities in life. To give you an idea of the type of thing I mean, here are mine, in order of importance: family, fitness, finance, learning and business. Family also encompasses my small inner circle of friends. Fitness is mental, physical and emotional. Finance pertains to personal cash flow and my overall wealth position. Learning is both for pleasure and within my profession. But what's important is that I'm abundantly clear on what my priorities are, and I refer back to them – and my values – each and every time I need to make an important decision.

You will, of course, probably have different priorities such as contribution, community, sport, hobbies, legacy, parenting, networking, productivity, safety or security, spirituality or faith. Take your time to explore your own personal and professional priorities. Getting clear on your top five will help you focus on what's most important when it matters most. Two things I think it vitally important to include in your priorities in some form are wellbeing and relationships. Because if we accomplish great results while neglecting our health and the people around us, then we're not really achieving high performance.

I think it's also important to approach your priorities with situational awareness. Different situations in your life or work will require you to be nuanced in how you tackle decision-making. Certain priorities might be weighted. If, for example, family is a top priority and it's your partner's 40th birthday party, then you might assign that a greater importance than a potential career opportunity on the same day. You need to be able to see the forest for the trees, so take the time to clarify what's *really* most important at any given moment. There will be times when your health might need a higher weighting, whereas other times it will be your career that needs your full focus.

Take your time with working out what your true priorities are. If you need to, write down everything you can possibly think of, then take a few days to whittle them down and double-check they are where your priorities truly lie.

In your journal, list your top five priorities, then make sure you rank them in order of importance, as I did with mine above. Whatever comes out at number one is your most valued priority (MVP), which we'll revisit and cover in more depth in Chapter 7.

Keeping your fire burning

High performers develop processes for making clear decisions. I created my values-and-priorities (VP) decision-making filter for just this purpose. I use it myself and I've passed it on to my clients. We'll take a look at it shortly, but the good news is that you've already done the heavy lifting by identifying your core values and your priorities. This already places you among a small number of everyday heroes who have radical clarity on their values and priorities.

I applaud you for doing the work to uncover what truly drives you at your core. Inside your mindset and heartset is a passionate, burning fire that brings your unique gifts to the people and planet around you. You are truly on the path to playing the high-performance game. So many potential high performers let that fire burn out by allowing their passion to be diluted by distraction. This non-essentialist approach leaves us struggling to go narrow and deep and instead we go wide and shallow. People stuck in this groove tend to say a little about a lot rather than a lot about a little.

We all have dreams, goals and aspirations, but when we let doubts determine our decisions, we downsize our destiny. Every day we have to make decisions, and with each and every decision we mould and shape our life.

Before I share my powerful decision-making filter, let's take a moment to look at the word 'decide'. Two syllables, de- and -cide. Take a moment to think about other words you know that end with -cide. I imagine some disturbing words might be popping into your mind: pesticide, genocide, homicide, suicide. The common thread in all of these words is the suffix that means 'to kill'. When we de-cide upon something, we are effectively killing off all other options and pursuing one. The word 'decision' comes from the Latin word *decidere*, from *de* meaning 'off' and *caedere* meaning 'cut'. In other words, to 'cut off' all of your other options so that you can commit to one. Next time you make a decision, remind yourself how crucial your process is. Each micro-decision you make will shape your macro-life. Your days are your life in miniature.

The decisions I've made in my life to date have been a combination of good, bad and indifferent. But each and every one of them has shaped where I currently sit in life: the house I live in, the family I have, the clients I serve, the adventures I experience. All these present-life conditions have been influenced by micro-decisions along the way.

THE VALUES-AND-PRIORITIES (VP) DECISION-MAKING FILTER

Take a look at the decision-making diagram on the next page. The top left quadrant holds your core values and the top right holds your priorities. Those parts are easy, because you already know what they are from the earlier exercises. The bottom left is reserved for the opportunities that you see arising from saying yes to the decision you're considering. The bottom right is a space to explore the potential costs of pursuing the decision. This is the VP decision-making filter.

VALUES	PRIORITIES
OPPORTUNITIES	COSTS

In their book *The Adaptive Decision Maker*, John Payne, James Bettman and Eric Johnson emphasise the value of writing as a part of a structured decision-making process. We gain significant clarity by getting out of our head and onto the page. These authors also stressed the importance of using structured approaches, such as decision matrices. Writing is a natural way to organise and structure information. When we write down our decision-making criteria and alternatives, and the outcomes of different options, we create a visual and systematic framework that helps us clarify our thinking.

If you'd rather join the masses in the short-game life, then just continue with busy being busy. But slow is the new fast, so take your time and let these high-performance models shape the next decade of your life.

The VP decision-making filter in action
How does the VP decision-making filter work in practice? Let me share two examples.

I was in South Africa travelling with my partner, enjoying the vibrant people and culture of Cape Town. While we were there I met with the leader of the Kolisi Foundation, a charitable organisation founded by the captain of South Africa's world champion rugby team, Siya Kolisi, and his then wife, Rachel. The foundation's vision is to change the stories of inequality in that beautiful country and see communities thrive.

When I spoke to the Kolisi Foundation, they kindly invited me to host a charity evening in London at the Spotify headquarters to raise funds and awareness. Siya's documentary film, *Rise*, would also be screened to the attendees. Everything about the event and the purpose behind it left me feeling like my decision would definitely be yes – it was a great honour and very humbling to be invited. I said yes 'in principle', which afforded me 24 hours to check my diary for existing commitments and priorities. A few hours later, I opened up my diary to discover that the day after the event in the UK, our son was going to be on stage in his first-ever school production in Christchurch, New Zealand. My heart sank, I really wanted to be at his first school play, but I also wanted to help this amazing organisation with its northern hemisphere event.

This is where my VP filter kicked in and allowed me to make a decision without the frustration, worry, anxiety, procrastination and indecision I used to experience before I had a proven model to support my decisions. Back then I would have said straight away, 'Hell yes, I'll book the flights.' But I've also experienced the pain and suffering caused by overcommitting and overpromising. And I knew how often that impacts both my loved ones and my own wellbeing. Of course I was conflicted. Being able to support Siya and Rachel's charity would have been simply incredible, but the thought of being absent from my son's first school production felt unthinkable.

Instead of making the decision based purely on emotions, I decided to get out of my head and onto the page. I detailed my core values, then wrote down my priorities in order: family, fitness, finance, learning and business.

I then proceeded to draw two VP filters using my core values and my priorities, combined with the costs and opportunities. I filled out one of these filters for attending my son's school production, and the other for the philanthropic event in London. It became abundantly clear that one decision far outweighed the other. Family sits right at the top of my priority list, and heading to the UK didn't add to that in any way whatsoever. From a physical and mental fitness standpoint, a 38,000-kilometre round trip to the UK didn't seem smart. And on the financial side, it would have meant cancelling a corporate speaking gig to which I'd already committed. Don't get me wrong, there were positives for going to London, particularly from a learning, brand and philanthropy viewpoint. But first things first. Family is my number-one priority, so I made the decision to attend the school production. The Kolisi Foundation fully understood, of course, and we explored other ways I could support its mission over the long term.

Simply knowing what my priorities are, and their order of importance, continues to help me make clearer decisions. I don't make perfect decisions every time, but I certainly make decisions that more often align with my values and priorities, and that help me move towards being the partner, father and leader I want to be.

The second example is from a client of mine who used the filter to help her get clear on an important decision.

Charlotte was the managing director of a large marketing company in Sydney, Australia. She was highly effective at her job, well respected in her industry and paid handsomely. But the co-founder of the business, who also happened to be an in-law, was not treating her respectfully. The situation was complex and challenging on many levels. I coached Charlotte through this challenge for several weeks and we got to the point where she needed to make a decision. The number-one rule for any coach is never to make the decision for a client. So I stepped her through the VP decision-making filter. Charlotte identified two options: stay in her current role, or resign and seek fresh pastures.

Charlotte's core values are honesty, excellence and respect. Her priorities are fulfilment, impact, family, wellbeing and personal growth. The opportunities she identified from staying in her current role included learning more about how to deal with conflict and developing tools for having courageous conversations. But the costs included a negative impact on her mental health, a significant negative impact given multiple family members were involved in the business, and a lack of personal growth as she was being held back from being innovative. I think it's reasonable to consider having two sets of values: one pertaining to your professional life, and the other to your personal life. But I firmly believe that complexity causes confusion. If your set of core values is strong, you should be able to apply it to all areas of your life, so you can show up as your authentic self in each and every setting.

If she decided to resign and seek new career options, the opportunities would allow her to meet her need for fulfilment by growing and learning. This option would also enhance her wellbeing, as she would be moving away from the drama with her in-law who was also a co-founder. That in turn, would help her maintain better familial relationships over the long term. But the costs would involve potentially lengthy time off work and a possible drop in salary.

As she weighed up both options, she felt the data and her gut instinct begin to align. It became clear to her that the decision to resign would allow her to stay true to her core values of honesty and self-respect. The opportunities involved in resigning were also stronger than those that would come from staying.

The VP filter might seem like a methodical and mathematical approach to decision-making, but it often results in an emotional outcome. Charlotte called and told me of the huge sense of elation she had experienced when she resigned. It was life-changing for her, and the great news was that *she* made the decision using an objective tool.

The next time you need to make a decision, draw the VP decision-making filter in your journal and walk through the process. Getting out of your head and onto the page will help you make clearer decisions and elevate your performance in the short and long term.

STAY

VALUES	PRIORITIES
• HONESTY • EXCELLENCE • RESPECT	• FULFILMENT • FAMILY • IMPACT • WELLBEING • PERSONAL GROWTH
• LEARNING MORE ABOUT CONFLICT MANAGEMENT • TOOLS FOR COURAGEOUS CONVERSATIONS	• NEGATIVE IMPACT ON MENTAL HEALTH • NEGATIVE IMPACT ON FAMILIAL RELATIONS • LACK OF PERSONAL GROWTH • LOSE SELF-RESPECT • LOST TIME SPENT WORRYING AND STRESSING
OPPORTUNITIES	COSTS

LEAVE

VALUES	PRIORITIES
• HONESTY • EXCELLENCE • RESPECT	• FULFILMENT • FAMILY • IMPACT • WELLBEING • PERSONAL GROWTH
• MEET MY NEEDS FOR FULFILMENT • GROW AND LEARN LOTS • ENHANCED WELLBEING • IMPROVED FAMILIAL RELATIONS • MORE SELF-RESPECT • BE ABLE TO MAKE A POSITIVE IMPACT ELSEWHERE	• LESS INCOME • TIME OUT OF WORK
OPPORTUNITIES	COSTS

Principle 5: Get out of your head and onto the page

Let's bring it all together. Too often we try to get granular before we make a move. We want to plan every minute detail before we take the first step. We want to work through every possible eventuality before committing to action. And that's why we live in a world where a large number of people are settling for mediocrity in their careers, relationships, health and wealth. Procrastination, indecision and fear are the dominant traits of many, and it keeps them stuck in a horrible holding pattern. You've got to land that plane and get on with it. If the rubber doesn't hit the tarmac, you'll end up being a shoulda-coulda-woulda kind of person.

This might be the single most important component of being a high performer. If you nail this, the rest will follow. Too few people take the time to get radically clear on their vision, and instead spend so much time on devices that they get caught with a large dose of digital dementia.

What we're *not* going to do right now is make a detailed plan. We're not going to write out the step-by-step action list of how you're going to win by playing with a high-performance edge. Success leaves clues, no matter what part of life or work we look at. The greatest performers and humans all have certain ways of approaching their biggest dreams, and I fully believe they have a recipe that we can follow. To put it another way, there's no need for us to try to reinvent the wheel.

Know your end game

The first thing successful people get clear on is what their end game looks like. In other words, what their version of success looks like.

Marc Allen is a friend who shared his story on my podcast, and it's a great example of getting out of your head and into your heart.

He awoke on his 30th birthday to find his life wanting. He was living in a slum apartment with no job, no money and a history of failed careers. He barely scrounged his rent together each month and scraped by.

'On my 30th birthday, I decided to take it up several levels,' Marc told me. 'In fact, a quantum leap in what I was visualising. And so, literally, I spent most of the day alone, pacing up and down. I couldn't have the party, I just needed to think about my life because I was 30. This voice said, "You're not a kid any more. You're 30." Somehow at 29, it was cool to be a musician, unemployed, with no money whatsoever. But turning 30 really changed me.'

Four specific actions altered the trajectory of Marc's life that day:

1. He wrote down his *ideal scene* over the next five years and identified that he would have a successful publishing company, despite having no prior interest in business. He also decided he 'would live in a big, beautiful home in Marin County [San Francisco, California], with a beautiful view.'

2. From his ideal scene, he identified *specific goals* that would help him achieve that vision. 'I would start learning about publishing companies and start learning about real estate. Start writing a book.' These goals were his stepping stones towards achieving his ideal scene over a five-year period.
3. He turned his goals into *affirmations*, writing them down and repeating them to reinforce his new mindset. He used the phrase 'in an easy and relaxed manner, in a healthy and positive way, in its own perfect time, for the highest good of all' with each affirmation.
4. He began creating *simple, one-page plans* for each of his goals, starting with basic steps like reading a business textbook and talking to people who knew more about business than he did. It was not unlike the simple approach to entrepreneurship we see from Richard Branson, the founder of Virgin, and Steven Bartlett, the founder of Flight Group.

By the end of that year, Marc had already started his publishing company, with a small catalogue and a couple of books. His first-year sales were $800. In the second year it stretched to $3000. But with patience, conviction and commitment, he built an enduring company that has made millions of dollars. Marc co-founded New World Library, one of the largest publishers of spiritual books on the planet. Some of the books he has published include bestselling titles: *The Power of Now* by Eckhart Tolle and *The Seven Spiritual Laws of Success* by Deepak Chopra.

Marc's story is an example of getting out of your head, into your heart and onto the page. When we're stuck in our heads we tend to procrastinate. Marc managed to transform his life by having a simple plan and sticking to it.

Now it's your turn. And as we embark upon this vital step in crafting a life you're sublimely proud of, let's keep it simple. Get out of your head, and into your heart.

We all need an Altair

On any journey, it's critical to have something strong to guide us in the right direction. For millennia, humans have used stars for navigation. The brightest star in the constellation Aquila is Altair. It symbolises balance and navigation, and features in the myths of various cultures for its role in celestial wayfinding. It's easily visible to the naked eye and can be found high in the sky in both hemispheres from July to November. Altair rotates rapidly, and so is often associated with speed and dynamism. For me, it symbolises the idea of progress.

Altair helps to ensure that an explorer ends up reaching their final destination. In the context of high performance, our metaphorical Altair is our big personal goal. It will serve as a steadfast inner compass amidst life's change and uncertainty. Our Altair is something that remains unchanged for an extended period of time. It inspires us, challenges us and motivates us to take massive transformative action over

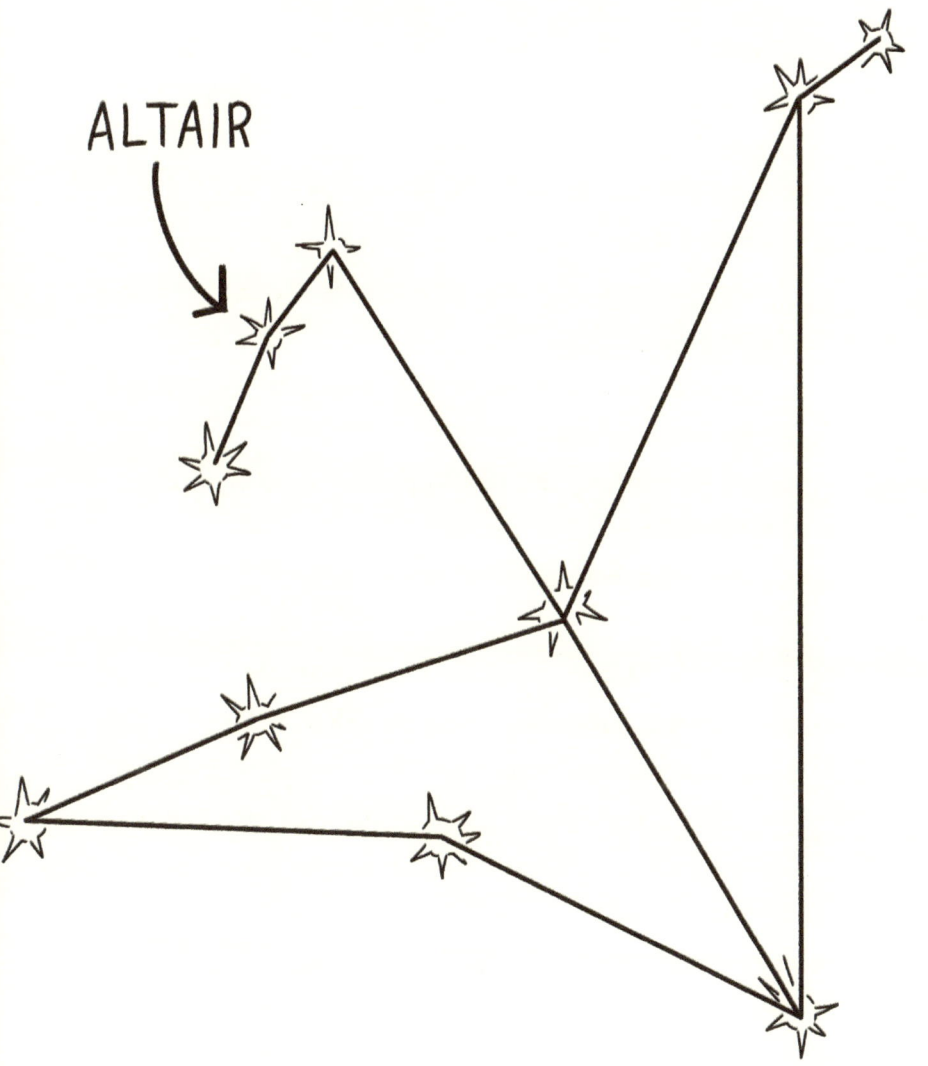

many decades. Our Altair symbolises a long-term, idealistic future state.

I mentioned earlier that success leaves clues, so let's look at a few examples of people who have set inspiring Altairs:

- Nelson Mandela: 'I cherish the ideal of a democratic and free society in which all persons live together in harmony and with equal opportunities.'
- Mother Teresa: Care for the poorest of the poor.
- Eckhart Tolle: 'Accelerate the awakening of human consciousness to create a more peaceful and harmonious world.'
- Simone Biles: Facilitate access to education for children from foster families
- Roald Amundsen: Be the first person to reach both the North Pole and South Pole.
- Richard Branson: 'Screw business as usual.'

What do you notice about all these examples? They are all succinct, to the point and inspiring. This is the approach we want to take when setting our Altair – something that will keep us taking big swings day after day, year after year.

What if you reach your Altair sooner than you think? Great! You can set a new one. But most people take a lifetime to reach their vision, if at all. If you end up reaching your Altair after a few years, perhaps you haven't set your sights high enough.

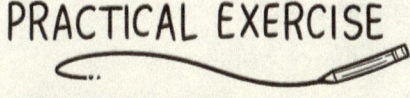

PRACTICAL EXERCISE

SET YOUR ALTAIR

Let's equip you with your own Altair. You might have a single Altair for your career, sport, health, community, relationship and wealth. You could have a number of them. All I'm asking you to do is to pick one in an area of your life in which you're committed to being best-in-field. In what part of your life are you willing to play the long game?

Naturally, this can be a difficult task to complete, so you probably need a little help. Here are a few guiding principles to help you.

Step 1: Explore what makes you tick

Grab your journal and answer the following questions. Go deep and wide with your answers. Remember, you're trying to get out of your head and into your heart.

- What keeps me up at night?
- What angers me about people, society and the world?
- What is a dream I think is impossible to accomplish in my lifetime?
- What makes me cry with deep sadness when I see it or think of it?
- What could I do for hours and never get bored?
- What topics do I like to talk about passionately?

- What would make my grandparents/ancestors proud?
- What has held me back in life or work?
- If I could be the world's greatest in one area, what would it be?

Step 2: Start crafting your Altair

Now that you've taken the time to explore your inner thoughts, frustrations and dreams, you'll be in a much better place to identify your Altair. And remember, your Altair may evolve over the years. Think of it like choosing a colour. Let's say you choose blue today. Well, over time your preference might change from royal blue to light blue to navy blue to azure, but the colour is still blue. Your guiding star will still be your guiding star, but just know that it can evolve.

Some ways you might start your Altair statement could be:

- To create ...
- To solve ...
- To be the first ...
- To end ...
- To provide
- To empower ...
- To reach ...
- To achieve ...
- To be named ...
- To give ...

Step 3: Formulate your Altair

Decide on the area of your life that you want to create your Altair for, then write it in your journal and formulate your Altair. Make it compelling, game-changing, daunting and inspiring. Try keeping it to one sentence at most.

If it helps, here's mine: To help great humans become the greatest in their chosen field of endeavour. In other words, my guiding mission is to help amazing people reach their full potential. Elevating others is my greatest passion. Staying committed to that outcome keeps me focused on my overarching mission each and every day.

Step 4: Keep your Altair front and centre
Congratulations. Seriously. If you actually completed this critical first step of a high-performance life, then you're among the small percentage of people who will actually do so. Grab five colourful sticky notes and write your Altair down on each. Pop those notes in five different locations around your house, car, journal and office. Surrounding yourself with what truly inspires you will ensure you never forget what gets you out of bed in the morning.

The great servant leaders of humanity never had to consult their iPhone to jog their memory for their guiding star. Mahatma Gandhi, Harriet Tubman, Nelson Mandela, Malala Yousafzai, Ruth Bader Ginsburg. What unites them all is their undeniable clarity as to what they stood for. They all played the long game and they were all radically clear on their Altair.

You are embarking upon a high-performance life, and because of that, you and I are deeply connected as mission-driven messengers. Please take a photo of your sticky note and tag me @jameslaughlinofficial on Instagram or @jameslaughlincoaching on LinkedIn.

From Altair to El Capitan

Knowing your Altair elevates you to the rare air of visionary humans, but you might now be feeling a little stuck as to where to begin. I call it '33rd step syndrome'. Before you start, it's easy to get stuck in the scenario where you're thinking of your first, second, third, fourth, right up to your 33rd step ... It's all so overwhelming that you become paralysed, overcome with the daunting reality that you can't make a dent in your journey towards your ultimate mission, so why even begin?

It's all very well to have a clear guiding star, but you have no hope of getting anywhere without a concrete goal you can focus on accomplishing. The great humans and organisations who have shaped society have all realised one important thing: pick a clear mountain to climb. Jim Collins famously called it a BHAG (big hairy audacious goal), others will call it a mission. I call it your El Capitan.

El Capitan, nicknamed El Cap, is a metaphor for a mammoth goal. It's a massive granite monolith in Yosemite National Park, known for its steep and nearly vertical face. Scaling it is considered one of the most challenging feats in rock climbing, requiring a best-in-field skillset and mindset.

The people who successfully ascend El Cap often take years to plan and prepare. Training is slow and gradual, and sometimes the climb requires multiple repeated attempts. It's not dissimilar to the process of working towards a personal or professional long-term goal, where progress is often slow and speed bumps are part of the journey.

Reaching the summit of El Cap isn't just about physical prowess, it requires careful planning and strategising. It also requires the ability to navigate problems and surprises. This epic climb demands physical endurance as well as the necessary mental resilience to overcome obstacles and fear. It's no different from the mental toughness required to pursue any other long-term ambition.

Your long-term goal (your El Cap) should be an unreasonable challenge that will require sustained effort, mental toughness and a radically clear vision over a long period of time. Anything that brings a significant feeling of satisfaction always requires a great deal of effort. Summiting your own El Cap will be a feat worth fighting for.

Many people who have tried to ascend El Cap have died en route. Yet some have triumphed over this mammoth, sheer rock face. It will likely take you ten to twenty years to climb to the top of your own El Cap, and there's a very real chance you might not make it to the summit. If your goal doesn't scare you, and if there's no chance of you falling short, then you're not setting a big enough goal. It should be borderline impossible to accomplish. Back yourself, and know that high performance is yours for the taking.

To help you shape your El Cap, here are some real-world examples:

- Noah Lyles: 'To be the fastest runner of all time.'
- Martin Luther King Jr: 'A world where my children would not be judged by the colour of their skin, but by the content of their character.'
- Samuel Whitelock: 'To become the most capped All Black of all time.'

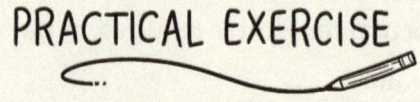 

PRACTICAL EXERCISE

CHOOSE YOUR EL CAPITAN

Now it's your turn. What would be a huge leap towards your Altair? A milestone towards accomplishing your life's purpose? It should be something that you know will take you anywhere from ten to twenty years to accomplish. Take some time to write the things you want to achieve, then narrow them down to get to your El Cap. Remember that it must be borderline impossible.

Once you've picked an El Cap, write it down in your journal. Writing it down makes it real. It's now a personal commitment. You're well on your way to playing in the rare air of the long-game high performer.

Now that you're radically clear and committed to high performance, join me on the next critical step towards greatness – supercharging your belief systems. The world is relying on you now more than ever. Your best self is exactly what the world needs more of.

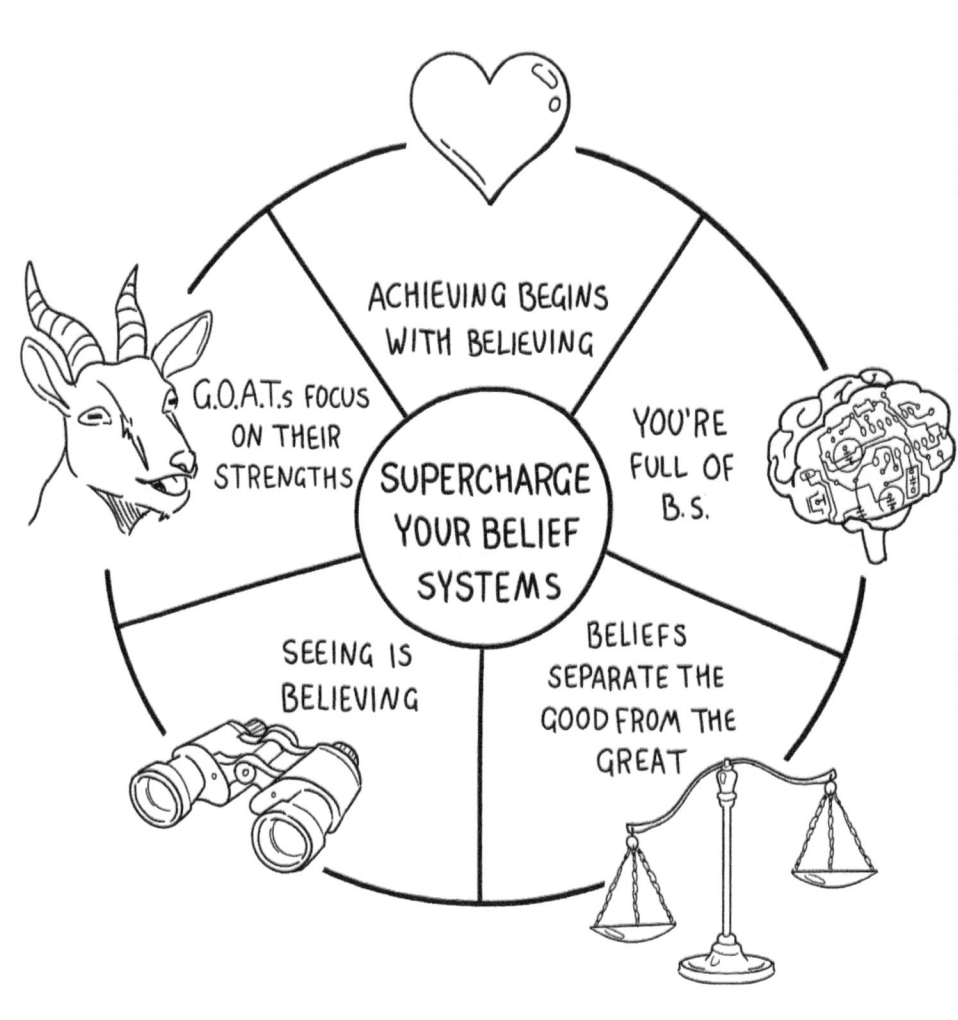

2
SUPERCHARGE YOUR BELIEF SYSTEMS

High performers achieve consistent results due to a small number of critically important habits. One of the most impactful habits they embrace is to supercharge their belief systems – which from now on I'll call their BS. We are all full of BS, which often stems from childhood and the ideas and truths that are imparted to us by parents, teachers and society.

Good performers and leaders generally have good beliefs, but high performers always have *empowering* beliefs. What separates the great from the greatest is a simple set of inner beliefs. These beliefs shape high performers' emotions and their actions. In the end, when someone isn't performing at their best, we can often trace it back to a limiting belief.

Success starts in the mind's eye. Seeing is believing, whether it be health, wealth or success in any realm. When you can clearly picture your desired outcome, it's much easier to move towards it.

Our beliefs either empower us to move towards our goals or they disempower us and practically paralyse us. The good news is, beliefs can be changed and rewired – and we're going to explore how you can do that. This will help you on your journey to becoming a high performer in every aspect of your life.

By the end of this second chapter, you will be equipped to supercharge your BS. We're going to explore the following principles:

6. Achieving begins with believing.
7. You're full of BS.
8. Beliefs separate the great from the greatest.
9. Seeing is believing.
10. GOATs focus on their strengths.

Principle 6: Achieving begins with believing

What do you imagine when you think of someone from Ireland? Humour me for a moment and just let your mind wander. What comes to mind? Perhaps it's St Patrick's Day, leprechauns, Guinness, 'Fiddle dee dee, potatoes', lucky charms, a great rugby team. Whatever comes to mind reflects your beliefs. It's important to define our mindset as a set of beliefs that shape how we make sense of the world around us.

Anything we repeat over and over will eventually become a belief. The great thing about beliefs is that you can change them by consciously programming your subconscious – with self-talk, mantras and affirmations.

Beliefs are the acceptance that something exists or is true, often without proof. Often this includes faith or absolute confidence in something or someone. Many billions of people have believed in a god they have never met. The same goes for billions of children and Santa Claus. People have beliefs about entire nations, often labelling them as bad drivers, aggressive or dumb, or making a plethora of other prejudiced judgements.

Who shapes our beliefs?

What we consume, we become. And I don't just mean the food that we eat is shaping our health. The words we listen to from our family, friends, mainstream news and social media all have a profound impact on our beliefs. A great example is the democratic election process. How many times have we seen it deeply influenced and shaped by false claims and social media? Many voters have been manipulated into believing certain narratives simply because they saw them on social media, or a relative or shock jock said they were true.

From an early age, we are meaning-making machines. We're constantly attaching meaning to experiences, which in turn shapes our belief systems. Our primary caregivers, siblings and relatives are therefore the people who impart values, norms and religious beliefs to us. This societal culturescape is forced upon each and every one of us, and it's up to us to challenge those norms if we want to be high performers on our own terms.

Religion, politics and education also play an integral part in shaping our belief systems, but as adults, two of the most dominant factors impacting our everyday beliefs are:

1. our peer group
2. social media.

Our peer group

Albert Bandura, one of the world's most respected psychologists, developed social learning theory. Entrepreneur, author and motivational speaker Jim Rohn summed it up in this simple statement: 'You are the average of the five people you spend the most time with.' With his famous Bobo doll experiment, however, Bandura gathered the psychological data that proves our beliefs and behaviours are a direct result of the influence from other people.

The study aimed to investigate whether social behaviours, particularly aggression, could be acquired through observation and imitation. It involved 72 children (half male, half female) between the ages of three and six from the Stanford University nursery school. They were divided into three groups:

1. **Aggressive model group**: who observed an adult behaving aggressively towards an inflatable doll of Bobo the clown. The adult hit, kicked and verbally abused the doll.

2. **Non-aggressive model group**: who observed an adult playing calmly with other toys and ignoring the doll.
3. **Control group**: who were not exposed to any behaviour with the doll.

After observing the model, the kids were placed in a room with toys, including a Bobo doll, and their behaviour was observed. The children who observed the aggressive model were significantly more likely than the kids in the non-aggressive and control groups to imitate the aggressive actions and verbal abuse towards the Bobo doll. This imitation was observed in both boys and girls, though boys showed more physical aggression.

The Bobo doll experiment offers compelling proof of Bandura's social learning theory, showing that behaviours can be learned simply by observing others. This study underscored the powerful impact that observation alone can have in shaping our beliefs and behaviour. It highlights the significant role that media, our social environment and our role models play in moulding our beliefs and actions.

Who we surround ourselves with, we become. We consume their ideas, thoughts and beliefs. If we don't consciously manage our surroundings and curate the type of people we want to be with, then who we are is less in our control. And studies prove that we start to think and act like the people we spend the most time with.

In recent years, I sat with the chief operating officer of a Fortune 100 company in North America. She was a most fascinating leader, passionate about people, and had stood up for what she believed in. She was responsible for 100,000 employees under her watchful guidance. During our conversation, she said, 'James, please tell me about the people you spend the most time with.' It became apparent that the majority of the people I socialised with were of a similar age, background, gender and ethnicity to me. She reassured me that this is quite common the world over; we tend to gravitate to people who look, think and talk like us. But it doesn't set us up to play the long game with a great deal of success. In fact, she highlighted that my lack of diverse social connections meant I had developed a mental blind spot, because nobody was able to challenge my thinking. I was living in an echo chamber – similar-thinking friends echoed anything I shared outwardly back to me. Confirmation bias, therefore, was clearly a huge flaw in my character set – the things I thought seemed true because everyone around me thought the same.

Following that chat with this amazing leader, I set about changing my social landscape by engaging with people who walked, talked and thought very differently from me. For a moment, please think about the five people you spend the majority of your time with each and every day. Who are they? Is there enough diversity in your personal social circle? If not, you're setting yourself up for some short-game shortcomings. You want to play the long game, right?

Social media

Behavioural scientist at Stanford University's Behaviour Design Lab, Professor BJ Fogg, developed persuasive technology designed to influence patterns of attitudes and behaviours in digital environments. His model classifies three elements necessary for persuading someone towards a desired behaviour: motivation, ability and trigger. Motivation is managed by feeling and includes pleasure or pain, hope or fear and social acceptance or rejection. Ability – the ease or difficulty of performing a behaviour – is influenced by time, money, the amount of physical and mental effort required, our degree of social conformity and how the behaviour fits into our routine. The trigger element is an external stimulus that leads us to the behaviour.

Engineers and designers have used models like Fogg's to manipulate our minds and our behaviours in apps such as Instagram through deliberate habit-forming techniques. Essentially, it makes these social media platforms addictive. The model was so effective that Fogg earned the nickname 'The Millionaire Maker'. These platforms make more money when you spend more time on them – by feeding you content that taps into our internal triggers, they drive us to check them compulsively and relentlessly. This, in turn, shapes our beliefs and behaviours across every aspect of our lives, including political persuasion, how we perceive physical beauty, what we aspire to own or buy, and so much more.

Researcher and bestselling author Johann Hari penned a compelling book on the pandemic of digital addiction and distraction. *Stolen Focus* took me to the dark depths of what is happening to our minds, and to humanity itself, all because of the addictive technology that was conjured up at Stanford.

If you're committed to being a high performer, then taking charge of what you focus on in the digital world is non-negotiable.

What role do beliefs play in our life and work?

When I was growing up in Northern Ireland, a small country that has been torn apart for decades based on people's beliefs, it was apparent that Catholics and Protestants were at war. Yet when you dig under the surface a little, you'll see that it's only a very small number of extremists who cause most of the unrest. When you step inside the homes of these people you can see that they are reciting rhetoric that has been passed down by parents, grandparents and beyond. In fact, when you start to ask some basic questions about why they hate the 'opposite' religion, they mention nothing about Christian beliefs and rarely, if ever, mention God or Jesus. The murals they paint are mostly of masked terrorists, freedom fighters or militant martyrs.

Generations of young Northern Irish people have been radicalised by the words their caregivers and family members shared around the kitchen table. I recall believing at one point that I could identify a Catholic because their eyes were closer together than those of a Protestant. I was six at the time, but it was a real, deep-seated belief that I'd heard hundreds of times in my school playground. My parents never dragged us along to church, and nor did they have opinions about people's religious beliefs. This falsehood greatly impacted my belief system over the years. Just think for a moment about how many millions of people have been killed over their beliefs in something, or someone, that nobody has ever seen. If an alien race were to look down from above, I imagine they'd be scratching their heads (if their anatomy allowed it) in bewilderment.

Believe it or not, your beliefs play a significant role in shaping your thoughts, behaviours and actions. This happens in several ways, with differing levels of impact on your life and the world around you:

- **Decision-making**: Beliefs are often the foundational drivers of the decisions we make. You will consciously and subconsciously make decisions that are consistent with your inner beliefs.
- **Behaviour**: Religious or moral beliefs are an example of adherence to beliefs dictating or shaping people's behaviour. For example, a vegan might decide that they won't support the local cafe that serves animal products, or allow their child to attend a school trip to the zoo.
- **Perception**: Think of your beliefs as a lens, or pair of glasses, through which you see the world around you. It will determine what you notice, what you delete, what you interpret and, most importantly, the meaning you assign to your experiences.
- **Motivation**: When you have strong beliefs about something in particular it can be a huge intrinsic motivator, which drives you to act and pursue a meaningful goal.

Psychological frameworks offer many opportunities for looking at how beliefs shape us. A useful model is the belief-attitude-behaviour model, which is a somewhat holistic representation of a number of the most common social psychology frameworks. It shows how our beliefs directly influence our attitude, which in turn drives our behaviour, as follows:

1. Beliefs – our personal convictions that certain things or people are true and real – are the foundational component of the model. Beliefs are often based on personal experiences, family traditions, education or cultural norms.
2. Beliefs directly shape our attitude towards something or someone. For example, if someone believes that alcohol is not beneficial for meaningful relationships, they may have a negative attitude towards social events held at pubs or bars.
3. The action we take based on our attitude is what we define as our behaviour. Expanding on the previous example, the negative attitude towards alcohol-centred activities might lead to more of a focus on enriching experiences with friends, such as hiking or team sport.

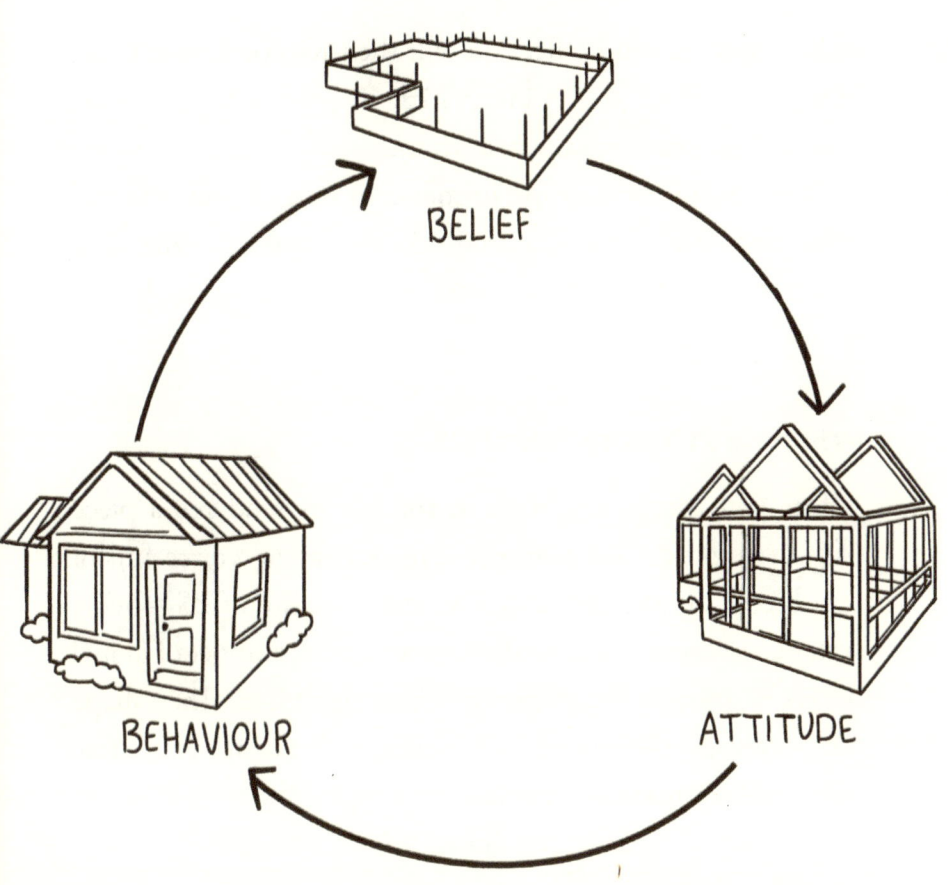

Whatever your beliefs, they are shaping your attitude and therefore your behaviour. This means that when you start to introduce empowering and positive beliefs, you create a positive feedback loop. For example, if you believe that journaling will help you manage your emotions and uncover your purpose, then your attitude to journaling will be positive and open, which will shape your behaviour of writing each morning. The positive results you enjoy after days and weeks of introspection and reflection will then reinforce your belief in the benefit of journaling, which in turn will strengthen your attitude towards the behaviour.

If you want the high-performance results in your life and work, then it's crucial that you take the time to rewire your beliefs so that they support your mission. Achieving begins with believing.

Principle 7: You're full of BS

Before you throw this book in the bin or send me a piece of your mind on social media, I'm not saying you're full of bullshit. Quite the opposite. You and I are full of BS – belief systems. Every moment of the day, we have a number of global beliefs running through our subconscious mind. They shape our actions, feelings and behaviours, and essentially dictate how we show up in the world.

One way of categorising global beliefs is to look at them in broad-brushstroke groupings:

- **Self-beliefs**: individual opinions about yourself, others or the world around you, based primarily on your lived experience.
- **Religious or spiritual beliefs**: opinions that often involve faith, doctrines or practices.
- **Scientific beliefs**: opinions based on empirical evidence, which may change as new information emerges.
- **Political beliefs**: ideas and opinions about government, distribution of power and policies.

- **Cultural or social beliefs**: opinions shaped by the customs and traditions of the community that has surrounded you.

Your perception shapes your reality. You make sense of the world around you through your personal filter, which is moulded by your belief systems. What reality looks like to you might be vastly different from how it looks to somebody else. One of the greatest sources of human conflict for many millennia has been the diversity of beliefs and how passionately entire societies defend their stance.

Self-beliefs: The seed of sabotage or success

The key to high performance is understanding your self-beliefs. You need to uncover your beliefs about yourself, the people around you and your purpose here on earth. I work with everyday people who want to become the greatest version of themselves, and I'm very attuned and alert to the language they use. When people come to me with problems or obstacles, I often sit and listen, because the words they use to express themselves outwardly are a mirror of their inner feelings and beliefs. Often they see roadblocks as external forces, but for the most part they are inner challenges.

People are often their own greatest obstacle, but the great thing is that, more often than not, the obstacle *is* the way. What I mean is, when we move towards an obstacle and start to consider the possibilities, we begin to find a way to overcome it. The only way to grow is to overcome the obstacle in front of you.

Self-limiting beliefs are one of the greatest barriers in the worlds of business and sport. Andrew Blackman, a former *Wall Street Journal* staff reporter, described them as, 'assumptions or perceptions that you've got about yourself and about the way the world works. These assumptions are "self-limiting" because in some way they're holding you back from achieving what you are capable of.'

Before we attempt to step towards our Altair, we need to get clear on our inner self-beliefs – because otherwise we are hamstringing ourselves from the outset. What happens within dictates what unfolds without. The thoughts you focus on inside your mind have a significant impact on your life in the physical world. Your mind is the single greatest determining factor in whether you reach the summit of your El Cap. If I could wave a magic wand over you and increase your chances of reaching your personal summit tenfold, would you want me to? Well, I'm about to do exactly that, and it's easier than you might think.

Principle 8: Beliefs separate the great from the greatest

Over the years, I've discovered that high performers can unlock success by rewiring four specific beliefs:

1. success
2. failure
3. money
4. happiness.

Supercharge Your Belief Systems

These are the most common areas that accelerate people towards their El Cap or stop them before they even take the first step. Here are some excuses I've heard over the years from clients, friends and most certainly myself. Never forget that beneath every excuse there is always a self-sabotaging belief:

- 'I'm too busy.'
- 'I'm too old.'
- 'I'm too young.'
- 'I come from a family of big-boned people.'
- 'Money doesn't grow on trees.'
- 'I don't have the money.'
- 'I don't have the resources.'
- 'I'm a night owl.'
- 'I'm not a morning person.'
- 'I don't like to read.'
- 'I'm too fat.'
- 'I'm too slow.'
- 'I have a bad memory.'
- 'I don't have a network of influential friends.'
- 'The world doesn't help people like me succeed.'

And the list goes on. Have you said any of the above? I most certainly have. I remember looking at successful people and thinking, 'I could never achieve that.' I came from a working-class town. I wasn't a trust-fund baby. I didn't have a private-school education ... My list was literally endless. Until my beliefs were challenged. Reading great books and seeing underdogs win was what truly rewrote the narrative of what I believed. I realised that high performance is a choice. And it begins with you choosing how you define your beliefs.

A family member told me often in my childhood years, 'Money doesn't grow on trees.' I know it was their way of trying to get me to be careful with money, to value money and to ensure I didn't get money-hungry. But they were passing on their beliefs about money and they didn't have an abundance of it. So I was only really hearing beliefs from one side of the money story. Did it hold me back? Yes! For many years I didn't see myself earning much more than a minimum wage. I thought my life as a waiter was the height of my station. I didn't know how to manage money, never mind investing it. I was stuck paying bills month by month. Then I read a book that transformed my money mindset: Mark Hansen and Robert Allen's *One Minute Millionaire*, followed closely by Napoleon Hill's *Think and Grow Rich*. That's it, two easy-to-read books transformed everything for me.

My young son, Finn, was with my partner, Caroline, and me on a family trip back to Northern Ireland. When a family member said at one point, 'Money doesn't grow on trees,' Finn instantly piped back, 'Yes it does.'

Our relative, who was trying to instil their money beliefs in Finn, really pricked up their ears. 'What do you mean?' they asked.

Finn replied, 'Well, my dad says that money grows on trees and never stops growing. He told me that my mind is the tree, and so long as I water it and feed it then it will keep producing lots of money in life.' I was sitting quietly in the corner trying not to burst into laughter. Finn continued, 'And Dad said if I always ask teachers and elders why, then I will continue to learn. And if I read every day and learn about the world, then I will always be feeding my tree. Maybe you could try it too?' At that point I broke into a quiet giggle. I was proud of Finn, and it was proof that beliefs can easily be instilled in others, and in ourselves. I hope Finn's beliefs about money serve him well, and inspire him to be a learner for life.

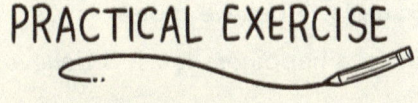

REWIRE YOUR BS

Are you willing to get radically honest with yourself? You're going to identify your current inner beliefs so we can rewire them if required and ensure you don't become one of the many who get stumped by the big four beliefs: success, failure, money and happiness.

Step 1: Decide

Grab your journal and take a moment to explore your BS. You're simply going to write down your current beliefs about each of the big four, then ask yourself 'Is my current belief deeply empowering and helping me become a high performer?' If your answer is no, I want you to write down what you feel would be the most powerful new belief. You don't have to believe it now, you just have to write it down. And then start to think about it, journal about it and say it every day.

Here are a couple of examples that might help you. My old belief about money was 'Money doesn't grow on trees' and my new belief is 'Money grows on trees, in abundance, so long as you water and feed the tree.' My old belief about failure was 'Failure is bad and results in letting others down' and my new belief is 'Failure is my shortcut to success.'

When trying to figure out what your current beliefs are, simply start with the 'I believe …' prompt and let your pen run wild. For example, 'I believe money is …', 'I believe success is …', 'I believe happiness is …', 'I believe relationships are …'

Use your journal to capture your old beliefs and new beliefs, perhaps using this table format if you find it helps.

The big four	Old belief	New belief
Success		
Failure		
Happiness		
Money		

Step 2: Get the reps in

Well done on taking a moment (and it takes a lot less time than you might have imagined) to decide which beliefs you want to rewire. But deciding won't make any difference unless you install those new beliefs at a subconscious level. You need to turn your new beliefs into personal mantras that will help you bridge the gap between simple words and deep-seated beliefs.

Repetition quite literally breeds belief. Research shows that repeating information influences its perceived truthfulness. Psychologists Aumyo Hassan and Sarah J Barber studied the phenomenon known as the illusory truth effect and found that repeated information is often perceived as more truthful than new information due to increased processing fluency. This effect persists even when people are aware that the source is unreliable or when the statement contradicts their own prior knowledge.

Here's how it might unfold in the real world. Repeatedly hearing myths such as 'People only use 10 per cent of their brains' or 'The Great Wall of China is visible from space' can lead people to accept these statements as true, even though they have been debunked by experts. Other oft-repeated claims like 'Eating carrots improves your eyesight' or 'Cracking your knuckles causes arthritis' can lead people to believe these health myths, despite a lack of scientific evidence.

Whatever you repeat to yourself, you begin to believe. A meta-analysis combining the results of numerous studies found that athletes who engaged in positive self-talk techniques showed improvement in their performance across multiple sports. This is because it helps them

> to visualise success and manage stress, which jointly contributes to better physical and mental outcomes during competitions.
>
> Later in this book you'll learn to implement a powerful set of mantras that will help you reinforce your new beliefs about your own life and your goals.

Mind your language

The modern era has brought with it a modern language – or should I say a lazy language. Humans like to shorten words and adapt words from urban slang, but we need to realise that language plays a prominent part in shaping how we feel and act.

How about describing that world-class figure-skating performance as 'sick'. Or that sublime gelato you had as 'dope'. Or wishing a friend luck for an exam with 'Go crush it'? How about telling a colleague to 'Kill it' with their upcoming public speech?

Scientific studies show that positive and negative words not only affect us on a *psychological level*, but also have a significant impact on the outcome of our lives. Using painful or negative words increases implicit processing within the brain, which simply means that our stress and anxiety levels can be increased by the words we decide to use. When neuroscience proves that our use of words can dictate our level of psychological stress, that's a pretty compelling reason to choose the high road with our language.

Supercharge Your Belief Systems

Neuroscience has shown that words can literally change your brain. When you hold a positive and optimistic word in your mind, you stimulate frontal lobe activity. To impact the world around you in a positive way, the positivity must start within. Your self-talk is the seed of self-mastery. Choosing to use exquisite words and sublime language will have a compounding effect on your mindset, your emotions and your behaviours.

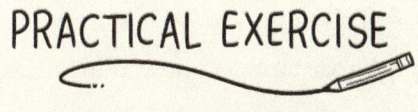 

PRACTICAL EXERCISE

LEVEL-UP YOUR LANGUAGE

If you want to play the high-performance game, then you need to commit to a language level-up each and every day.

Step 1: Listen to yourself carefully

The first step in levelling up your inner dialogue is to become aware of the words you use, out loud but especially in your mind. For the next 24 hours, I want you to take stock of the words you're using to describe yourself, your abilities and your actions. Are they uplifting words? Do you swear frequently? Do you use vulgar language? Pay attention to that little voice in your head to see what it's saying.

Step 2: Replace your negatives with positives

Each time you identify a negative word, my challenge to you is to replace it with the most sublime word you can muster. When you actively start to look for the optimistic slant in everyday challenges, you begin to rewrite the neural narrative inside your head. This is the starting point for every action you take.

I catch myself frequently reverting to negative self-talk, and negative descriptors about situations, events and people. We all possess a negativity bias, an ancient survival mechanism that helped our ancestors stay alert to physical threats and dangers, which is largely redundant in our relatively safe modern landscape. We have thousands of thoughts every day. It's important to know that more than 85 per cent of what we worry about never happens and 97 per cent of our worries are baseless. In short, it's paramount that we take the time to focus on what is positive and what is possible. If we don't take charge of where our focus goes, it will naturally revert to worry and rumination. Where your focus goes, your energy flows. The price of entry to the realm of high performance is being actively focused on our language.

When I do find myself saying negative words, or thinking them, I implement a rule of replacing each one with three positive words. Negativity has a longer shelf life than positivity because of nature's hard-wired design of the nervous system. Scientists have discovered that it takes three positives to counteract one negative experience. So for every awful experience you endure in an activity or from a person, you need to experience at least three positive emotional experiences to counteract that. Dr Barbara Fredrickson, a positivity researcher at the University of North Carolina, coined the term 'three-to-one positivity ratio' and says, 'The potential for life-draining negativity lies within you, just as does the potential for life-giving positivity. You have more say than you think about what you feel and when. The treasure for your own positivity is waiting.'

Step 3: Level up your language daily
High performers know that practice makes permanent. Get started today. Pay attention to your thoughts and spoken words, and when you hear a negative one, simply replace it with three positive words. Or if you speak negatively of another person, choose to find three things you admire about them. If something upsetting, frustrating or disappointing happens to you, then seek to create three positive experiences throughout the day. The micro-wins *are* the macro-wins. Don't set yourself up for disappointment. Keep your positives to something very achievable: perhaps it's carving out five minutes to meditate, or watching the sunset, or reading a book for 20 minutes, or savouring a hot drink. Look for the gold in the small moments to truly take ownership of your positive psychology.

Principle 9: Seeing is believing

An old mentor once told me, 'What you can hold in your head, you can hold in your hand.' It was an odd concept and a little obscure for me, but then I started practising a simple yet powerful exercise he shared with me. I'm going to share that exercise with you shortly, as it can be a transformational tool for your high-performance life.

First, though, I want you to picture a young boy sitting at the back of his school classroom. He can't sit still and he has to be the centre of attention. One day he turns the gas on in all of the Bunsen burners in the science lab, knowing the smell will annoy his classmates. A teacher tells his mother, 'Your son will never be able to focus on anything.' In his book *No Limits*, the man this young boy became describes himself as follows, 'I had big ears. I was scrawny. And I got picked on a lot.' The young boy who many felt would amount to nothing in life harnessed his ADHD to help him become the greatest of all time in his chosen endeavour. His parents divorced when he was seven years old, which meant he needed to find something to grab his father's attention. His older sisters were swimmers, and so he started swimming too, begrudgingly at first as he hated it. As time passed, however, he began to enjoy it. 'Once I figured out how to swim,' he says, 'I felt so free. I could go fast in the pool, it turned out, in part because being in the pool slowed down my mind. In the water, I felt, for the first time, in control.'

This young boy's coach taught him relaxation techniques so he could visualise success in the pool. 'Once you get in a relaxed state, it's like watching a movie,' the coach told him. 'Sometimes it's like you're sitting in the stands watching yourself swim.' The boy would visualise his swimming strokes, entire races and his goggles filling with water, painting the most flawless performances in his mind's eye. This emotional visualisation became a significant part of his daily training.

For a moment, picture this. It's the 200-metre butterfly final at the 2008 Beijing Olympics, and this boy has now grown into a man. He's mid-race and his goggles fill with water. But he has mentally rehearsed this hundreds of times. Instead of panic, he knows what to do and wins his fourth gold medal at the games while setting a world record. What he could hold in his head, he could hold in his hand. By now you've possibly figured out who I'm talking about: Michael Phelps. He's the most decorated Olympian of all time in any sport, having amassed 28 medals overall (more than the entire Olympic medal count of 161 countries) – 23 gold, 3 silver and 2 bronze.

If Michael had listened to the teacher who said he would never be able to focus on anything, then we may never have witnessed the greatest swimmer of all time. He knew what his Altair was, and set several El Caps throughout his life. His ability to visualise the end game was one of his greatest strengths.

You too will have naysayers and critics, but never let them deter you from dominating your domain. Neuroscientists and researchers have confirmed in many studies that visualisation can have a marked impact on our ability to achieve success. Charles Duhigg, in his book *The Power of Habit*, writes that 'for habits to permanently change, people must believe that change is feasible'. So when you embark upon personal visualisation, it's important for you to truly believe that summiting your El Capitan is achievable. Studies show that people who mentally train by imagining themselves flexing a muscle as well as physically training that muscle achieve greater physical strength gains than people who engage in physical training alone. If you take the time to visualise your performance, skill or routine, then you will improve your chances of success.

PRACTICAL EXERCISE

VISUALISE YOUR FUTURE SUCCESS

Step 1: Create your vision

First, let's get out of your head and onto the page. Explore each of the questions below and write as detailed answers as you can in your journal.

1. What is your El Cap? Write down what success looks like at your summit.
2. Who can you see celebrating with you?
3. What else can you see?
4. What can you hear at the summit?
5. What can you feel, either on your skin or perhaps in your hands?

6. Are there any smells you are aware of?
7. Is there a taste you associate with this victory?
8. Are there any specific physical actions involved in you reaching your summit?

Now you have the basis of a very powerful and precise mental visualisation. Read, add to or edit your notes. Keep this journal close, because it's something you will want to refer to frequently.

Step 2: Practise visualising

Now practise your visualisation with your eyes closed. Perhaps re-read your notes three or four times before closing your eyes. Pop on some brown noise if that's helpful, or at the very least create a space that is private and quiet.

Take a comfortable seat or lie down flat. Start by focusing on your breath, simply noticing your belly rising and falling. As your mind starts to think random thoughts, keep returning it to your breath. Relax any muscular tension. After a few minutes, picture yourself reaching the summit of your El Cap. Use all of your senses: sight, sound, taste, touch and smell. Go through the physical actions you might have to perform, and see yourself doing them flawlessly. As you picture yourself in this movie, believe that world-class is truly possible. Michael Phelps's coach told *Forbes* magazine, 'He smells the air, tastes the water, hears the sounds and sees the clock. If you can form a strong mental picture and visualise yourself doing it, your brain will immediately find ways to get you there.'

> Repetition is the key to success, so it's important to make this a daily habit. (Later in the book we will explore how to install the habits that will give you an extra-competitive edge in your high-performance life.)

How visualisation helped me become a world champion

If I go back in my mind to 12-year-old James, I recall lying on my bed each night visualising my El Cap. I wanted to become the World Solo Pipe Band Snare Drumming Champion in the Juvenile grade. I had no business with such a big dream, as nobody in my family had a track record as a musician. But I believed that through hard work, clarity and daily execution, it was possible. Each night, I did exactly what my mentor taught me: I would visualise myself stepping onto the stage in front of the adjudicators in the World Championship final. I would see my dad in the crowd, I would feel the smooth wooden drumsticks in my hands, I would hear my feet tapping as I prepared to perform at a specific tempo, and I'd smell the fresh wood of the drumsticks I had selected just before performing.

I would then go through every part of the performance in painstaking detail. It was a three- to five-minute performance with several thousand micro-details, dynamic articulations and permutations. I would see myself playing the most intricate rudiments with ease and feel confident, even as my hands started to sweat under the spotlight and my sticks started to slip. I would visualise every possible eventuality so that when the time came I was prepared to do what was required. Often, during my visualisation, my mind would wander to what I was having for lunch at school the next day. Not very helpful, but also a reminder to get back to focusing on the task at hand. I then went back to the very beginning of the mental performance. Doing this daily led to a strong sense of self-belief. I knew I could perform at a level good enough to be considered for the world title.

Making visualisation a daily practice is something that high performers prioritise, time and time again. Continue to march to the beat of your own drum, and embrace this one-percenter routine.

Imposter syndrome

High performers still have doubts and fears. They still wonder if they can really make it to the summit. Whenever I've sat down with high performers – be they country leaders, dignitaries, elite athletes or industry titans – the vast majority have asked me one thing after our interview or panel discussion on stage: 'James, was it okay?' They wanted to know if they had performed well enough. They wanted to know if what they shared had any value or worth for the listeners.

That sense of humility can also cross into the territory of self-doubt. Many of the greats I have coached or worked with have talked about imposter syndrome. One study found that imposter syndrome is common among high-functioning, high-achieving individuals, and also highlighted how important it is to reduce or diminish this behavioural health problem. If imposter syndrome is left to fester, it can contribute to many detrimental effects, including comorbidities such as depression and anxiety. If you're wondering whether you experience imposter syndrome, here's a definition from researchers in the field. In their paper 'Imposter Phenomenon', Martin Huecker and his co-authors say: 'Self-doubt of intellect, skills or accomplishments among high-achieving individuals. These individuals cannot internalise their success and subsequently experience pervasive feelings of self-doubt, anxiety, depression and/or apprehension of being exposed as a fraud in their work, despite verifiable and objective evidence of their successfulness.' Can you relate to that? I most certainly can.

A few prominent personal examples of experiencing imposter syndrome stand out for me, including my career transition from James the drummer to James the high-performance leadership trainer. Until then, my whole identity had been that of a drummer. I struggled to see how I could coach people in how to develop the skill set, mindset and heartset to achieve high performance in fields other than music. Another example was the first time I did a live interview with an audience, and my guest was a former world leader. Until that point I had conducted hundreds of interviews and received positive feedback from audiences and listeners the world over. But this was a former prime minister. 'Should I do things differently now?' I asked myself. 'Should I write out questions?' I wondered, even though I never wrote out questions. 'What if he thinks I'm a crap interviewer? What if the audience sees that I'm a fraud?'

All of this self-talk was running through my mind on the morning of the event, so my partner asked me one simple question: 'What would you do to help a client in the same situation you're in?' She was my coach that morning, that's for sure. I realised the answer was simple: I'd ask them to remind themselves who they are and get out their personal victory journal.

The power of the personal victory journal (PVJ)

As humans, we all experience some level of self-doubt, and this phenomenon won't disappear anytime soon. One recurring theme I've discovered over the years is that the vast majority of elite performers have some form of highlight reel to which they can refer when they need to remind themselves that they are capable. When you feel like quitting, or not even starting, it's really useful to have a tool that can help you maintain your forward momentum.

In an interview with Tom Bilyeu on his podcast, *Impact Theory*, former Navy Seal and now bestselling author David Goggins describes his 'Cookie Jar' method. Essentially, he takes all of the failures, suffering and achievement through adversity that he has experienced in his life and puts them into a 'cookie jar' in his brain, 'Because in times of suffering, even the hardest men forget how hard we really are.' Whenever Goggins gets pulled into a 'woe is me' or 'life sucks' mentality, he says he goes to that cookie jar to remind himself what a 'badass' he really is: 'It's a reminder of who you truly are at the core of yourself.'

I've had clients who've called it a 'brag book' – somewhere they record their victories so they can reflect on them when they doubt themselves the most. No matter where you are in life, at some point you have had to overcome adversity or challenge. It might be surviving school, learning to tie your shoelaces, learning to read, buying your first car, learning to ride a bike, getting your first job, meeting your first intimate partner, traversing the loss of a loved one or a relationship, dealing with financial struggle, battling an addiction, speaking in public ... the list goes on. Whatever you have overcome, write it down somewhere.

PRACTICAL EXERCISE

YOUR OWN PVJ

Creating your personal victory journal is simple. Grab your journal (or you could make a note on your phone) and start to reflect on the moments in your life and career where you've accomplished something that required you to truly push through your own limitations and doubts.

Go back through your life and capture all of the moments you can think of – perhaps do a few each day for the next month until you have an extensive list. I like to take screenshots of client feedback, or a testimonial from someone who has hired me to speak at their event. I then pop those in a photo album on my phone so the next time I'm feeling nervous or doubtful, I simply look through those photos.

> Let's be clear, though, this is not meant to be an ego trip. This is meant to be a powerful tool to take you from self-doubt to self-belief. If you can't believe in yourself, why should anyone else?

Celebrating your micro-wins

When I'm working with a professional sports team, I always tell them to ensure they maximise their celebration of the tiniest wins on the field – a good pass, a penalty won, securing space or a goal. The size of what you've done doesn't matter, what matters is that you start to build that emotional muscle. Off the field this could be the equivalent of completing a task on your daily to-do list, learning a new skill or making a positive lifestyle change (like drinking one less coffee, or actually doing your five-minute meditation).

To summit your El Cap, look for small wins. Karl E Weick, a renowned organisational theorist and professor at the University of Michigan, believes that a small win is 'a series of concrete, complete, outcomes of moderate importance'. Ticking off that tiny item on your to-do list may seem insignificant, but Weick says that these small wins begin to reveal 'a pattern that attracts allies and deters opponents'.

I have personally witnessed a professional sports team I was coaching turn an entire game around through the power of micro-wins. They were on the back foot from the outset, and by half-time were down seven points. Things weren't looking good, but they decided to use the midpoint to reset their focus. They decided that concentrating on the tiniest victories was crucial to taking control of the game. In the second half they doubled down on celebrating each good pass, each successful tackle and each point. They did this for an entire 40 minutes and came out on top. Your life off field is no different. Whether it's the hill you're trying to ascend on your bike, the book you are trying to write or the savings goal you've set, they all seem like far-off outcomes and can be so daunting that you quit. But when you can focus on celebrating the tiniest progress, you start to build the mental momentum to persist. El Cap is best climbed one step at a time.

Your PVJ will be your personal method of capturing the micro-wins you've had throughout your life, so don't stop adding to them. This simple process of celebrating each one will impact your self-image and consequently your beliefs, feelings and behaviours.

Principle 10: GOATs focus on their strengths

When it comes to supercharging your BS, it's important to look to the greatest of all time, those who are the best in their field. When you look at a high performer – be it a great athlete, a revered military commander or a respected CEO – you will begin to see a pattern of focus: they focus largely on identifying their strengths and doubling down on them. Of course they're still aware of their weaknesses, but they spend less time fixing their weaknesses and substantially more time strengthening their strengths. If you don't know what your strengths are, then you're at a disadvantage from the outset, and your chances of climbing your El Cap are greatly reduced. Over the next few pages, we're going to uncover your personal and professional strengths. You will then be aware of what makes you unique, and you will most definitely have greater confidence in who you are.

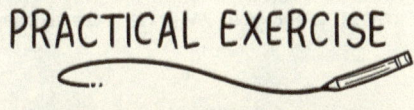 

LEARN YOUR STRENGTHS AND TOP TRAITS

My annual in-person self-leadership programme includes my top traits exercise. Participants have to get their phones out. That's right, I ask them to get their digital distraction devices out for a moment, right in the middle of the course. I want you to do the same thing right now. What you're about to do may feel a little uncomfortable, but I've had thousands of people, just like you, do this exact exercise, and it's had a lasting positive impact on each and every one of them.

Step 1: Ask for feedback

I want you to consider sending the following text to eight to ten of your friends, family and past or present colleagues. It's important to only send this to people with whom you share a mutual respect. You're going to send this text so that you can understand what others see as your top traits. Seeing our own strengths can sometimes be difficult. As I like to say, the contents of the jar can never read their own label. The solution is to ask someone outside the jar to tell you what it says.

Type this message and send it to your chosen people. When you get a response, simply respond with a sincere 'Thank you'. Be prepared for some wisecracks or jokes, but rest assured that for the most part you will get genuine and inspiring feedback.

Here goes:

> *Hey! I'm focusing on some important areas of my personal leadership and growth. Can I please ask you to support me by sharing an honest response to the following question?*
>
> *If you could extract one trait from me and implement it in your life or career, what would it be?*
>
> *Much gratitude*

When you get each response, please record these top traits in your journal.

Once you start receiving that feedback from friends, peers and family, I would encourage you to sit with your feelings for a moment. Often at my live events, people can become quite overwhelmed with joy and a little emotional at the feedback. Embrace those feelings. Your emotional connection to your strengths, and what other people around you perceive as positive traits, will be crucial in playing the long game on the way to your Altair.

Step 2: Identify your innate strengths

The second step in identifying your innate strengths is something that more than 30 million people have taken part in: the CliftonStrengths survey, by Gallup Inc. This is one of the most respected personal strength self-assessments and I have used it for myself as well as for my clients. It's a very small investment, with a significant ROI. To take that assessment, head to the downloadable resources by visiting www.jjlaughlin.com/habitbook

Knowing your strengths and top traits is simply the starting point. It's what you *do* with that knowledge that actually matters. The high performers I've had the pleasure of coaching and mentoring all have a way of bringing out their strengths on a daily basis. They also push themselves to grow and expand in those specific areas. If you're committed to playing in the rare air of greatness, then building on your strengths will be non-negotiable. The community leaders, athletes and titans who are known are those who nurture their talents unabashedly. It's your time to double down on your self-belief and start that next step towards your El Cap.

I've met great humans who know what their Altair is, have identified their next El Cap and have massive levels of self-belief, and yet they still struggle to stay the course through the long game. You've started to develop a high-performance mindset, and I salute you, but now it's crucial that you develop a high-performance *heartset*. Life will throw ambushes at you, and you will need emotional juice to stay in the fight.

Let's take the next step in your monumental journey.

3
LEAD YOUR LIFE ON PURPOSE

High performers who play the long game require a deep connection to something much bigger than themselves. You will inevitably encounter turbulence, speed bumps and potentially even life ambushes as you ascend your El Cap en route to your Altair. The people who uncover what truly drives them and identify their 'why' are those who persist in the face of adversity. They are the everyday heroes who continue to fight the good fight. People who lack connection to a deep purpose, on the other hand, are often those who suffer from shiny object syndrome (SOS). They are on their way to their El Cap when they see an interesting or lucrative opportunity and they jump at it. They continue to repeat this pattern of short-game behaviour until they realise a number of years later that their El Capitan has changed so many times they no longer understand where they're heading or why they're heading there.

To play in the rare air of greatness in your field or industry, you will need to be a *connected* high performer. Being someone who leads their life on purpose will enable you to say yes to what truly matters, and say no to the noise and distractions. High performers live life with what's most important at the core of everything they do. The most notable high performers I've coached and mentored all have a significant degree of self-focus. People around them might describe it as selfishness, but you and I, who understand the sacrifice required to reach the summit of our El Cap, know that this intense self-focus is necessary. It might mean that you spend fewer nights out socialising, or fewer hours on your couch consuming Netflix. And you might spend more time refining your craft, mastering your mind and maximising your genius. This is the greatest challenge for you and every one of us: to be able to stay focused on WMI. Tapping into your purpose will equip you with the emotional fuel you'll need to sustain your pursuit of mastery.

People at my seminars often ask me, 'What is purpose?' It seems to be this elusive and almost out-of-reach, intangible idea for many. Yet it doesn't have to be. We simply need an answer as to why we do what we do. But first let me point out that there's a notable difference between passion and purpose. Passion is for you, purpose is for others. What I'm saying is that passion – and you'll often have multiple passions in various parts of your life and over time – is something you indulge in for your own pleasure and joy. Purpose, on the other hand, is the sense of fulfilment we derive from doing things for others.

Passions bring you feelings of exhilaration, excitement, flow and reward. It might be a hobby like tennis, golf, windsurfing, snooker, knitting, chess, playing a musical instrument or art. You do these things because of the feeling you experience during and afterwards. They are rewarding endeavours and things you can do with others or individually. Passion is so important, as it adds depth and colour to life. Passion is truly a gift, and something we shouldn't take for granted. A successful life devoid of fulfilment is the ultimate failure. The number of world champions, Olympians and mega-rich people I've met who are deeply unfulfilled is countless, and what a shame. Life is a treasured gift to be enjoyed. Pursuing our passions is a crucial way for us to meet our needs for variety, connection and growth.

Having passions in your life will bring a degree of fulfilment, but we also need to experience *meaning*. One of the greatest ways to do this is through contribution, one of the core human needs that we'll look at in the next chapter. When we're focused on helping others, we're less likely to be focused on ourselves and our worries or problems. Purpose is for others. Too often in our modern era, I find that when people talk about their 'purpose', it seems to be more of a passion than a purpose. Purpose is about making a difference, looking outwards, not expecting recognition and truly giving your time, resources and wisdom. When you can tie purpose to the pursuit of your Altair, you've got a winning formula. When you've crafted a connected purpose, you're well on the way to winning the long game.

Finding purpose in your Altair might come easily. Maybe you're driven to eliminate a disease, end child poverty or lead a nation toward a better future. These altruistic Altairs are tied to a deep sense of meaning.

For others, purpose may seem more self-focused at first glance – becoming an Olympian, building a billion-dollar company, or being the best in your field. But even these aspirations can look outward. The athlete inspires the next generation. The entrepreneur creates jobs and transforms industries. The artist redefines how we see the world. The key is this: whatever your Altair is, it can and should serve something greater than yourself.

For many years I've hosted the *Habits of High Performers* podcast and interviewed a whole range of amazing high performers. At the end of every episode I always ask them what advice they would give to someone who wants to lead their life on purpose. I've noticed some recurring themes and patterns emerging from their answers. In this chapter, we're going to explore those themes and develop the habit of leading your life on purpose by looking at the following principles:

11. Do work that matters.
12. When your why is clear, your how is easy.
13. Purpose is the high performer's edge.

Principle 11: Do work that matters

A story that demonstrates the power of a purpose-led life is that of Nigerian-born, Duro Oye. Duro was shipped off to London at just five years old to live with his sisters, as his mum felt it would provide him with more opportunities. What she didn't realise, however, was that his older sister was living in a council estate and working day and night. His sister's boyfriend exposed Duro to things that no child ever should be exposed to. Duro saw criminal activity as normal from an early age, and he embarked upon his life of crime at 12 years old. He ascended the ranks and put his own 'crew' together, growing his gang by nurturing and developing his innate leadership skills – in all the wrong ways. He was an effective communicator, had the ability to win people's hearts and minds, could paint a compelling vision and could guide people. He was truly leading them with his own skewed sense of purpose. When he turned 18, his mum moved to the United Kingdom from Nigeria and demanded that he attend university. This removed him from his toxic social circle, forced him to spend a lot of time in solitude, and gave him time to reflect.

When Duro and I spoke, he told me, 'I knew that if I continued on this life-of-crime path, there would be three options. One: a long stretch in prison. Two: be killed. Or three: serve time in prison and be deported back to Nigeria. I knew I was better than that, so I applied myself. And on August 16th 2006, I moved back to my mum's house in London to start over. There was no more hanging with that bad circle. I was called to help people that were on the same path that I was previously.'

Duro went on to found 20/20 Levels, an organisation that aims to improve the lives of black youths in London by teaching them the skills to become better individuals and gain access to employment in the corporate world. 'I calculated that I'd led 450 young people astray in a life of crime. I made it my mission, with 20/20, to help at least 450 young people lead a life of purpose.' At the time of writing, Duro and his team have now helped well over a thousand young people. His programme is set to go global, so that young people can see that there is a positive pathway. The renowned sneaker company Converse was one of the first corporations to partner with 20/20 Levels, and the programme continues to empower young black entrepreneurs by connecting them with global business leaders. Duro was able to hook his life's mission up to a large purpose that made a difference, and it has driven him to create a global movement.

Where you're from, how much you earn, who your parents are and your past mistakes do not define your future. You are not your past, unless you choose to live there. Whatever sits in your past does not have to define you. Perhaps your past isn't as bad as Duro's, or maybe it's worse, but just know that when you commit to helping others and a life that is purpose-driven, you will inspire a whole movement of humans who want to come along for the journey. It starts with identifying *your* purpose – not the purpose of your team or organisation, but your personal why. Let Duro's example be a reminder to do work that matters.

The purpose of purpose

As we dive into the idea of purpose, it's important to acknowledge that it comes in various forms:

- **Oxford Dictionary definition**: 'the intention, aim, or function of something; the thing that something is supposed to achieve'.
- **Stoic viewpoint**: Marcus Aurelius wrote, 'People who labour all their lives but have no purpose to direct every thought and impulse toward are wasting their time – even when hard at work.'
- **Psychological viewpoint**: Friedrich Nietzsche wrote, 'Those who have a "why" to live, can bear almost any "how".'
- **Personal or professional context**: Purpose can refer to desired individual goals and outcomes.

We want to incorporate a number of those views when constructing our personal sense of purpose. It's clear that having a purpose will provide many benefits – personally, professionally, in our relationships, and for our community and potentially the planet at large.

Although some people dismiss purpose-centred leaders as being soft, I would argue that those who are connected to a purpose are those who make the biggest impact while experiencing the deepest sense of meaning. The soft stuff is the hard stuff.

Eddie Jaku published his first book when he turned 100. *The Happiest Man on Earth*, which details Eddie's experiences in his younger years, transformed millions of readers' lives. Eddie always considered himself a German first, a Jew second. He was very proud of his incredible country, but all of that changed in 1938, when he was arrested, beaten and taken to a concentration camp. He faced years of torture and unimaginable hell in Auschwitz. After he made it through, he vowed thereafter to smile every day.

As I read Eddie's book, I experienced many moments of deep sadness, anger, joy and hope. Despite the horrific things that happened to Eddie, including losing most of his family and friends, he believed he was now the 'happiest man on earth'. As you embark upon clarifying your purpose, I want to share with you one particular sentence from Eddie that really stood out for me: 'I had learned early in life that we are all part of a larger society and our work is our contribution to a free and safe life for all … Your efforts today will affect people you will never know. You can choose every day, every minute, to act in a way that may uplift a stranger, or else drag them down. The choice is easy. And it is yours to make.'

Eddie got it. He understood that a life well spent is a life that makes a difference to others. It is a life that focuses outward, rather than inward. Every human has experienced their own version of hell. Misfortune, trauma, loss and abuse are among the most common human experiences. Being able to navigate those experiences and come out the other side with a smile and a drive to make a difference is something truly remarkable. Eddie is a guiding light for us all. Finding your purpose in order to first ascend your El Cap and then ultimately reach your Altair is a challenge worth accepting. Will it be easy? Maybe not. But then again, most things worth fighting for don't come easy.

You decide what matters

Eddie is another reminder to do work that matters. But let's clear something up. Work that matters doesn't have to be charitable or community-focused. Work that matters should be defined by you and only you. If you're a barista, then perhaps you show up to be the best barista you can be, to make the experience for your customers more special. Perhaps you're a real estate agent and you see your role in selling houses as integral to bringing joy to the purchaser. Maybe you manage a small team, and you care deeply about helping each of them feel valued, so you go the extra mile to help them grow. This is doing work that matters. High performers do work that matters. It matters to them, to their El Capitan, and it keeps them motivated to stay the course.

Principle 12: When your why is clear, your how is easy

Once you take the time to get radically clear on your Altair's *why*, the steps for getting there will be almost blatantly obvious. Too many people try to start their 20-mile march to their El Cap without really knowing why they're marching there. And when a life ambush hits them, or a pandemic slams down on them, they quit. In business, the statistics back up this idea: 20 per cent of companies in America fail within their first year, 48 per cent falter after five years and more than 65 per cent of businesses fail after ten years. People who stay in the fight and play the high performer's legendary long game have a deep connection to their *why*.

An example of someone who was really clear on their Altair is Alice Law, co-author of *Unstressable*. Alice joined me on my podcast and shared her journey towards taking 1 million people per year out of stress. From the outside, you'd see a passionate and driven woman who is fully focused on delivering on her mission. But when you take the time to look underneath the hood, you'll see that Alice has a huge intrinsic *why*.

What on earth would inspire her to commit to such a mammoth El Cap? She had a wonderful childhood and all seemed relatively normal. Then the 2008 Global Financial Crisis came along, forcing her dad to put his business into administration and sell their family home. Her dad's identity was shaken, then legal proceedings against him multiplied his stress. Her sister was then diagnosed with colon cancer, which their dad struggled to come to terms with. 'Dad became very stressed and depressed,' Alice told me. 'He was using alcohol as his way to process. He didn't talk to anyone about it.'

Four days after her sister's funeral, Alice's dad was rushed to hospital. He had cancer all through his body. 'Whilst all of this was happening I lost my job and broke up with my partner. I then began to study stress and delved into all aspects of it.'

Four years later, her father passed away. 'It wasn't his cancer that killed him,' Alice explained. 'It was a burst stomach ulcer that caused internal complications accumulated from severe stress over a seven-year period. I went to see my dad in the funeral chapel, and as I was saying goodbye to him I thought, "I haven't seen him look that peaceful in years." I thought to myself, "This is not how life is meant to be for people."'

And so Alice developed her deep sense of purpose and embarked on a mammoth mission to set millions of people free from stress. She and Mo Gawdat, her co-author on *Unstressable*, are committed to diminishing the impact of stress on the lives of everyday people.

PRACTICAL EXERCISE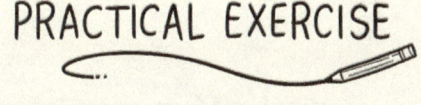

GO SEVEN LEVELS DEEP

A powerful exercise I've used for years, which has helped some of my most successful clients, both individuals and companies, is the seven levels deep exercise. You're going to take a moment to ask yourself why the Altair you're pursuing is so deeply meaningful to you.

The first answer that comes to mind is most often not the root reason we're driven to commit our life to a cause. I've conducted this exercise with a volunteer on stage in front of a live audience, and on several occasions it has culminated in tears and pure elation for that participant. Knowing why you do what you do allows you to focus on how you're going to get there. Nelson Mandela was radically clear on what he stood for, and he thoughtfully spent every waking moment pursuing his Altair.

Step 1: Drill down on why

First, grab your journal and write down your Altair. Now ask yourself, 'Why do I want to pursue that Altair?' Write down your answer, then ask yourself why your answer is important to you. Continue to ask 'Why?' for each answer you give, and do this at least five times. Take the time to do the exercise properly and identify your true why. The idea is to get to a point where you can't go any deeper with your why – you've reached the core of it.

Here are a few examples of how the process might look.

Sharon, a manager in the medical profession

My *why* is to be a great leader in the medical industry.

Why is leadership greatness important to you?
I believe everything rises and falls on leadership. And I want to help my team members and clients be the healthiest versions of themselves.

Why does helping others to be healthy matter to you?
I had a dad who worked all the hours God gave him. He worked overtime, he worked weekends and he even

continued to work when he got home for dinner. He had a heart attack in his late forties but he kept working hard. As kids, we didn't see him much. He then had a stroke at 54, which stopped him in his tracks. We lost out on the best years of life with him, as did he with us. My purpose is to help everyday people connect with their loved ones.

Why is connection important to you?
Connection is a deep core human need, not just a want. I see the damage caused by people who don't prioritise their health and their relationships. They may amass lots of wealth and status, but at the end of their life they are usually full of regret. I want to help others prioritise a blend of great health and rich relationships.

Why do rich and healthy relationships matter to you?
Life is short, and it's a one-time deal here on earth. Living a life rich in connection, health and meaning is at the core of everything I do. My north star is to help humans be the healthiest, most connected version of themselves.

And there we have it, only five levels deep and Sharon was at her core purpose: 'to help humans be the healthiest, most connected version of themselves'. It's simple but it's powerful, and you can see how the exercise helped her to dig deeper to what was really driving her to be the best in her industry. It was so much more than status or money; it was all about helping others experience what she lost out on with her own father.

Andrew, the real estate agent

My *why* is to be a top-five-ranked real estate agent in my region.

Why is professional success important to you?
I want to be seen as a successful and committed person. Being recognised as one of the top agents will make me feel proud.

Why does personal pride matter to you?
I have a young daughter and I want her to look at me with pride. I don't feel proud of myself at this stage in my career and I know that she won't feel pride for me if I don't feel proud of myself.

Why is family important to you?
I had a mother who made me, and continues to make me, feel that I'm not enough. No matter what I've done, or how hard I've worked, she never expresses that she's proud of me. It has meant that we don't have a positive relationship. I'm committed to ensuring that my daughter and I have a great relationship throughout my life. Being a top-five agent and bringing home good money will give my family the freedom to have choices.

Why does having choices matter to you?
I was always told that money doesn't grow on trees. And we never had much money when I was a kid, so we often lost out on opportunities because of our financial restrictions. I want to bring home more than enough

money so that I can provide my family with freedom, options and opportunities.

Why is freedom important to you?
As a partner and dad, it's the one goal that means the most to me. It's my responsibility and commitment. It will shape my legacy for my child.

After going six levels deep, it's clear that Andrew's *why* isn't to be a top-five-ranked real estate agent. It isn't about status or money, it's simply because he wants to create freedom for his family so they have options and opportunities.

Pablo, the breathwork and meditation teacher
My *why* is to make a living while not having to work 9–5 for the man.

Why is independence important to you?
I'm fed up working for a company that doesn't value me. They pay me okay, but they treat me like a number.

Why does significance matter to you?
Well, it's not significance from an ego point of view. I just want to matter. I want to feel like my work, and my presence, actually makes a difference.

Why does making a difference through your career matter to you?
I've helped a large organisation make a lot of money. But there's been a lot of sacrifice for me personally, with a huge negative impact on my relationships and wellbeing.

Why is wellbeing important to you?
My mum was a workaholic and it had the most horrible impact on our relationship, and it also meant that she got divorced three times. Her work-related stress contributed to her depression and anxiety. I started seeing the same red flags in my own health and relationship in recent years, and I wanted to take ownership of my choices. Life's too short, and I want to do work that makes a difference to others while it also fills my cup.

Why is fulfilment important to you?
I think that having a great career while lacking richness in my personal life is the ultimate failure. I want to experience satisfaction and joy in my professional life. Teaching breathwork and meditation brings me immense joy compared to my previous career selling widgets.

Pablo went six levels deep to realise that he wasn't making the choice to be self-employed because he hated working for the man. He was doing it because he wanted to experience satisfaction and joy in the work that he did.

Step 2: Keep your *why* front and centre
Write down your *why* on a fresh page in your journal. Each time I start a new journal, the first thing I write is my *why*. When I'm clear on that, my life flows so much more smoothly.

When your why is clear, your how is easy.

Principle 13: Purpose is the high performer's edge

But why all this fuss about *why*? People tend to get a little underwhelmed, bored or sceptical when it comes to digging around under the hood to identify their *why*. And if you're one of those people, I totally understand where you're coming from. Possibly you're a pragmatist and a realist, so you want to know why you should spend time identifying your purpose, and what benefits it might have in your life and work. Well luckily for you, I felt the same way several years ago and set off on a mission to figure out if there were enough reasons for me to pursue discovering my purpose.

The first thing I found out was that according to studies, people with a purpose live longer lives and outperform their peers, and have better immunity, less stress, better cognition and even better sleep.

Now let's tie that to your Altair and El Cap. If you have more brain power, get sick less, have less anxiety and live longer, your chances of achieving your mission will be higher.

Longevity

Premature death. How appealing does that sound? Not at all. In fact, I imagine you would do almost anything to extend your healthy life span. A growing body of studies is showing that people with a connection to a deep sense of purpose have better overall health and wellbeing and increased longevity. Researchers defined having a sense of purpose as having clear goals with a definite sense of direction. A study published in the journal *Preventive Medicine* in 2022 showed that people with the lowest levels of purpose were more than twice at risk of death as those with the highest sense of purpose. The study's lead author, Koichiro Shiba, an assistant professor of epidemiology at Boston University's School of Public Health, said, 'Having a purpose in life has been known to improve many health outcomes on average.'

When I turned 30, I became fascinated with the Blue Zones, geographic areas with lower rates of chronic diseases and surprisingly longer life expectancy. These zones have some of the highest concentrations of centenarians on the planet. If such places boast an abundance of citizens living healthily beyond 100 years old, surely they are doing something different. In association with *National Geographic*, journalist Dan Buettner set out to 'reverse engineer longevity'. Dan and a team of demographers studied longevity data and identified five regions where people are living much longer lives – Ikaria in Greece, Loma Linda in California, Nicoya in Costa Rica, Okinawa in Japan and Sardinia in Italy.

The study identified nine consistent patterns in all of the regions, which Buettner named the 'Power 9 principles'. People who live beyond 100 years old:

1. **Move Naturally:** live lives that encourage movement without conscious thought.
2. **Downshift:** take time in their day for rest and stress-free activities.
3. **Purpose:** know why they wake up each morning.
4. **Wine at 5:** drink alcohol regularly but only moderately.

5. **Plant Slant:** make plant-based foods the basis of their protein intake, and eat lean meats no more than five times a month.
6. **80% Rule:** stop eating when they are 80 per cent full, eat a small dinner early in the evening and make it their final meal of the day.
7. **Loved Ones First:** put their family first, commit to a life partner and invest time and love in their children.
8. **Belong:** are a part of a faith-based community and attend services regularly.
9. **Right Tribe:** are part of a social network that contributes to positive health behaviours.

I was excited to see that purpose is one of the nine core components of living a long life. What astounded me was that some of these geographic locations have a specific name to describe purpose: in Okinawa it's *ikigai* or 'reason for being', in Costa Rica it's *plan de vida*. Dr Robert Butler, the first director of the US National Institute on Aging examined the connection between longevity and having a sense of purpose. His work clearly identified that those who expressed a clear goal in their life lived longer and were cognitively sharper than those who did not. A study published in the *Journal of the American Medical Association* linked having a strong sense of purpose in people over 50 with a lower risk of death. The researchers found that participants who had the lowest life-purpose scores were twice as likely to die within a given time span than those with the highest scores. Purpose equals longevity.

Better immunity

People who are connected to a purpose tend to have a better immune system. This means they will have lower medical bills, spend less time at the doctor and enjoy a fuller life. A great example is Dr Steve Cole, professor of psychoneuroimmunology at the University of California, Los Angeles. When he was a postdoctoral researcher, having just completed his PhD, his unusual hobby was matching passionate art buyers with artists who suited their tastes. He had always loved art, so this allowed him to do something he deeply enjoyed while bringing joy to others and being remunerated. He says it gave him an extra layer of purpose and that he loved being able to help great artists.

When working at the university's Cousins Center for Psychoneuroimmunology, Steve started to wonder whether his quirky side hustle all those years earlier had actually impacted his immune system in a positive way. The studies he and his colleagues have since published suggest that negative mental states, such as loneliness and stress, influence gene expression and our ability to fight disease. The opposite is also true.

Author, speaker and entrepreneur Dr Joe Dispenza has overseen research that suggests we might upregulate and downregulate gene expression via our mental and emotional state. This could mean that our state of mind might turn certain autoimmune markers on or off.

Winding the clock back to my competing days, when I spent almost an entire year preparing for a seven-minute performance at the World Drumming Championships, I can recall a fascinating pattern. In the months leading up to the competition, I focused intently on this performance, often practising and rehearsing for more than 40 hours each week. The pursuit of the world championship gave me a deep sense of purpose. I was passionate about it, committed to it and willing to sacrifice a lot for it. On that journey to the world championship I felt those feelings of joy, flow and exhilaration that are common when we focus on our passions. Interestingly, I rarely, if ever, got sick during that nine- to ten-month build-up.

This is where it gets interesting, though. Almost every year after that, within a few days after the world championship, I came down with a chest or sinus infection. I recently requested my entire medical history from my doctor and it was mind-blowing to see the pattern of post-event sickness. I'm not alone in this: many of my clients who have been at the top of their game in global elite sport have reported the same experience after winning a world championship, the PGA tour or at the Olympics.

But why does this happen? According to Dr Nate Jones, a sports medicine physician at the Loyola University Medical Center, Chicago, doctors often refer to the 72-hour period after an intense event (which can be any event, to be honest) as the 'open window' for infection.

When we're focused on intense preparation, rehearsal or training, our body is flooded with the stress hormone cortisol, and the immune system reacts by going into defence mode. But once we've completed the performance or crossed the finished line, our immune response rapidly diminishes, leaving us more susceptible to infection.

A passionate purpose, something that we care deeply about, is much bigger than just us, and drives us to get up every day and keep moving towards our El Cap. This psychological and emotional drive has a notable impact on our biochemistry, flooding our body with feel-good hormones such as dopamine, serotonin, endorphins and oxytocin.

If you take the time to identify your Altair, the evidence suggests that your immune system will benefit. Imagine what this might mean for a CEO who spends her time helping all of her staff connect to a deep purpose. I suspect it would result in people taking far fewer sick days!

Less stress

Stress is a killer. The facts are damning. If you don't manage your stress, you'll need to manage your distress. When we're focusing on others, we spend less time focusing on ourselves. When we're committed to solving an existential problem for society, nature or the planet, we're less likely to spend time stressing about the laundry we forgot to do, the dishes left over from last night or the driver who cut us off on the way to work. In reality, though, we can't avoid stressful situations – life will continually ambush us with financial uncertainty, pandemics, natural disasters, and the loss of loved ones. But having a purpose in life can significantly impact our ability to reframe these stressful situations and deal with them more productively. This in turn helps us recover from stress or trauma.

One of my earliest leadership roles was heading up a competitive group of musicians aged from their mid-teens to their early fifties. To say it was stressful is an understatement. And I was under continual scrutiny from my peers and world championship adjudicators. I didn't have the full set of tools necessary for reframing the stress, and it soon compounded, leading me to consume a lot of caffeine, food and alcohol. I struggled to maintain composure and I had regular outbursts of passionate emotion. It felt terrible. At times I felt like my head or chest was about to explode and I was only in my twenties. It was clear that my purpose was no longer intact – in fact, it had morphed into more of an obsession with winning. Losing my sense of why I was doing what I was doing led to a surge in stress.

A metanalysis combining the results of several studies supports the idea that greater purpose in life is associated with less subjective stress. This is consistent across age, sex, race, ethnicity and education. So when I lost my connection to my purpose – why I was doing what I was doing – my personal stress levels skyrocketed. When you lose your why, your joy can die. Always search for that inner sense of meaning and purpose. Fight for it, journal on it, talk about it and share it. Purpose is the high performer's edge.

Research by Mo Gawdat and Alice Law, the authors of *Unstressable*, led them to conclude that there are four distinct types of stress:

1. **Mental stress**: which is present when you find yourself ruminating on the past or worrying about the future. Lack of sleep and lack of focus are often telltale signs too.
2. **Emotional stress**: which might show up in the form of Netflix overconsumption, overeating, low libido, tiredness and irritability.
3. **Physical stress**: which can present as headaches, shoulder and/or jaw tension, backache, hives, memory loss, high blood pressure and even heart attack.
4. **Spiritual stress**: which makes us feel disconnected from our intuition, lacking meaning and experiencing internal conflict.

What can we do? Well, high performers don't live a life devoid of stress, but they most certainly do have ways of managing it. Alice shared with me a simple strategy that might be useful for you on your journey. She made it clear that our emotions are at the root of it all. Her *Which, Where, Why, What* method is a pragmatic and powerful way of recognising and dealing with these emotions.

'Start with emotional curiosity,' Alice said. 'Befriend your emotions. Ask *which* emotion am I feeling? Then ask yourself *where* am I feeling it. Place a hand over the area on your body that you feel the emotion. Breathe into that area. Ask yourself *why* am I feeling it? Lastly, ask yourself *what* can I do?'

This approach to heightening your awareness of your emotions will give you great insights into your emotional wellness. The journey begins with accepting and acknowledging your full range of emotions. Studies show that most people identify with three key emotions: happy, angry and sad. But Professor Brené Brown has researched emotions extensively and identified that there are 87 of them available to us. Curiosity about your emotions will help you live a longer life and achieve better results in everything you do.

Better cognition

Have you ever known an elderly person who is as sharp as a tack? How is it that someone can be over 80 years old and yet their brain fires like it did when they were 20? One possible reason is that people who have had a purpose throughout each stage of their life will generally have better brain function. This purpose could be anything from being a present parent to helping change something in their community or volunteering for those in need. We are often told that sudoku and crosswords are the best prevention for cognitive decline, but science shows that having a clear purpose has a powerful impact on our brain health. Being connected with our purpose can help protect our brain by building stronger neural pathways, which helps delay decline in brain function.

For a moment, picture a man nearing 80 walking briskly for kilometres at a time with upright posture and strength in his stride. He's setting the pace for the 30-something who's alongside him. This same nearly-80-year-old man is deep in conversation about cognition, neurolinguistic programming, social media, spirituality and love. He also happens to be in the international hall of fame for karate, has released a number of music albums, is renowned for his graphic design and is one of the founders of the Red2Blue mindset used by many of the greats, including All Blacks, Gurkhas and many other high performers. This man, Renzie Hanham, is a dear friend and personal mentor. In his presence I feel inspired, connected and grateful.

As Renzie nears 80, he continues to look for places where he can be purposeful and add value. He still dons his karate gear, he mentors young aspiring athletes at a university, and he travels New Zealand equipping leaders with mental skills. All the while he's writing songs, designing artwork for authors and indulging in deeply connected time with his loved ones. He shared something that will always stick with me: where your focus goes, your energy follows. How true.

Renzie's focus is continually on service, adding value, loving and connecting. In my humble opinion, he's a purpose-driven high performer playing the long game. If you're a long-game player, be a Renzie. Get clear on your Altair and keep pursuing it with vigour and valour. Renzie could choose, like many other people his age, to sit in an armchair all day, waiting for his next meal. But he is full of purpose, meaning and passion.

Better sleep

How do you feel when you don't have a great sleep? Groggy, tired, grumpy, distracted, irritable, unproductive and even sad perhaps? Sleep has a significant impact on every area of our lives including our relationships, health and career. The compounding long-term effects of sleep deprivation and sleep disorders have been associated with a wide range of health consequences, including an increased risk of hypertension, type 2 diabetes, obesity, depression, heart attack and stroke. Sounds terrible right? In the United States alone, it's estimated that 50 to 70 million people suffer from a chronic sleep disorder that affects their health and longevity. A study from Northwestern University's School of Medicine in Chicago reported that people who had a greater sense of purpose also reported better sleep.

The US National Sleep Foundation suggests an average of eight hours' sleep per night for adults, which sleep scientist Matthew Walker says too many people fail to achieve. Professor Walker, the director of the Center for Human Sleep Science at the University of California, Berkeley, believes that 'every disease that is killing us in developed nations has causal and significant links to a lack of sleep'. Later in the book, I'll share some tactics to enhance your sleep, but for now just remember how much your sense of purpose will impact your sleep.

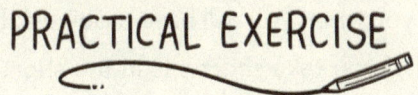

PRACTICAL EXERCISE

WRITE YOUR PURPOSE STATEMENT

The research and data reinforce that having a purpose in life is incredibly beneficial for our longevity, happiness, joy, relationships, health and so much more. And I can assure you that your odds of reaching your El Cap are greatly increased if it's tied directly to your purpose. To stay in the game over the long distance, it's crucial to take the time now to identify your *why*.

Step 1: Refine your purpose statement

Head back to your journal notes from Chapter 1 and take a look at your El Capitan and your Altair. Your purpose is the emotional driving force for stepping towards your ultimate goals, and you'll find that it bears a very close resemblance and connection to your Altair – it's a sibling of sorts. Take a moment to revise where you ended up with the seven layers deep exercise earlier in the chapter. This will be your purpose statement.

Step 2: If necessary, repeat the exercise with your Altair

If it doesn't feel like this statement fully resonates, then try the exercise again with your Altair as the starting point for questioning: 'Why is achieving my [insert Altair] important to me?' If you can distil into one cogent sentence the essence of what you're about, where you're headed and why it means so much to you, then you will have a powerful base from which to build. If you take shortcuts in the short game, prepare for short circuits in the long game.

Step 3: Keep reminding yourself of your purpose

On a fresh page in your journal, write down your Altair, El Cap and purpose.

> I would encourage you to write these weekly, as a ritual and practice. Remember that where your focus goes, your energy follows. Keeping your Altair, El Cap and purpose front and centre will help you make decisions that keep you moving towards your priorities.

You may have gathered by now that I'm interested in the origins of words and their meanings. Here's an interesting term: your brain's *frontal* lobe is home to areas that manage thinking, emotions, personality, judgement, self-control, muscle control and memory storage. By consistently writing down and talking about our goals and intentions, we keep them *front and centre* physically, but also psychologically and emotionally. Knowing that your brain is here to help you succeed, and learning how to work with it rather than against it, is valuable in helping you thrive.

So you now know where you're headed and why you're heading there, but what happens when you lose momentum, hit a roadblock, experience pushback, face criticism or listen to the naysayers? In the next chapter, I'm going to reveal the high performer's secret to staying the course on that climb to the summit.

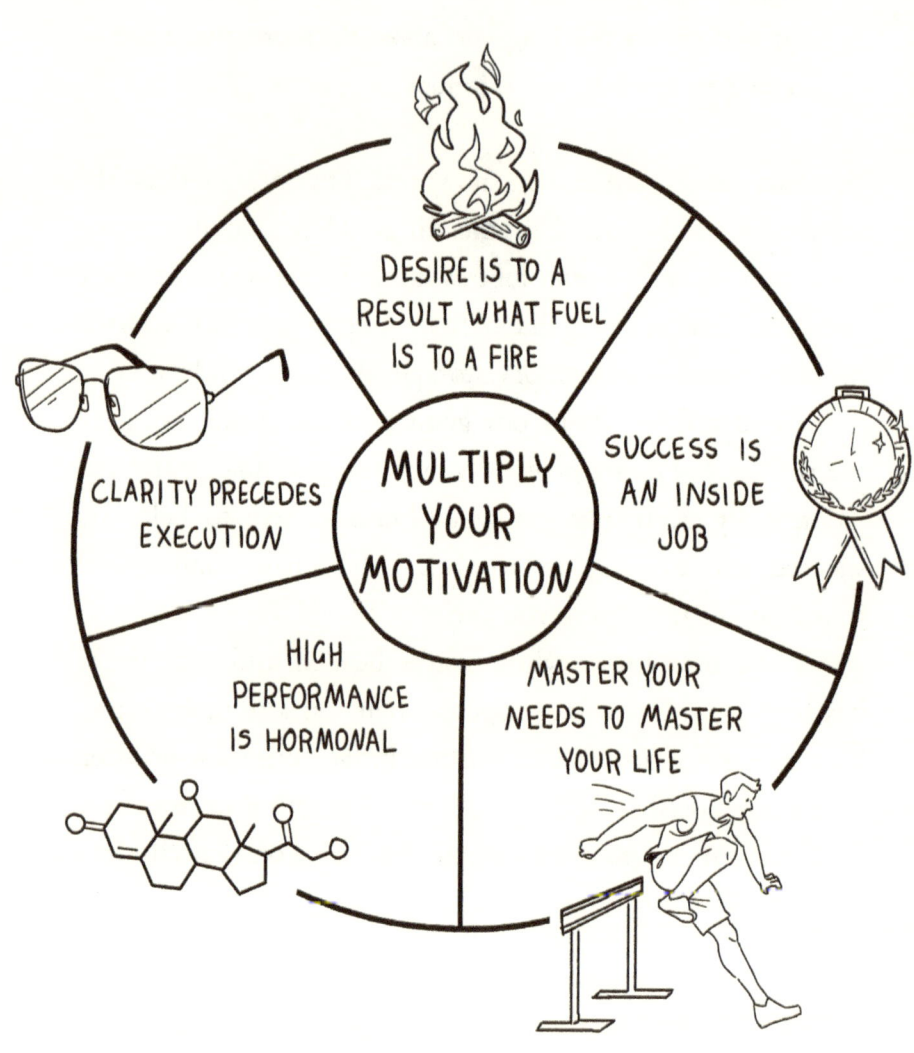

4

MULTIPLY YOUR MOTIVATION

If you're not compelled to act, you won't. If you lack the motivation to do the work when you're tired, then you simply won't do it. An awe-inspiring Altair and an exhilarating El Cap will become long-forgotten tales and coulda-shoulda-wouldas at the end of your life unless you tap into the emotional juice you need to take consistent action over the long game. High performers know how to access their inner desire and use it to propel themselves into doing the hard thing when they least feel like doing it.

We are living in a time when many are lauded for how easily they made their millions or how quickly they scaled up their operation so they could lounge about with their feet up. We seem to be surrounded by a generation of dreamers who think a four-hour working week is a common occurrence. But in my experience, those who pursue a lofty ideal and put in the consistent action required to make it a reality are the true game-changers. Serena Willams, Michelangelo, Richard Branson, Oprah, Beethoven. Each person is a household name in arguably every country on the planet. Do you think any of them lacked the ability to harness their intrinsic desire to accomplish greatness? They are among the finest performers the world has ever seen, and all have embraced a framework that all true high performers have in common.

I've learned, from years of working with and interviewing great leaders and titans of industry, that success leaves clues. Those little breadcrumbs left by the giants of art, sport and business are gifts to you and me, so that we can learn from their greatness. When I was in pursuit of my seventh world title, or when I was helping a team I coached to their twelfth consecutive national title, I continually looked towards the great heroes and role models to see what I could learn from them. We all stand on the shoulders of giants, so there's no use trying to reinvent the wheel. Whatever you're trying to achieve, somebody has already successfully ascended a similar El Cap. So why not look to others to see what you can learn?

By the end of this chapter you will have the tools you need to multiply your motivation. To do this, you will implement the following principles:

14. Desire is to a result what fuel is to a fire.
15. Success is an inside job.

16. Master your needs, master your life.
17. High performance is hormonal.
18. Clarity precedes action.

Principle 14: Desire is to a result what fuel is to a fire

As a youngster, Jason Redman dreamed of becoming a US Navy SEAL. He was inspired to join one of the world's most revered elite special forces team and fight for his country and the freedom of suppressed civilians. Getting through BUD/S training, in particular 'Hell Week', challenged Jason to access his inner warrior just to survive without ringing the bell recruits use to signal that they are quitting. A huge percentage of SEAL trainees ring the bell before the end of the training programme, but Jason held on to his dream. He was one of the few who passed and graduated as one of America's toughest combatants. His journey with the SEAL unit took him to many places on the planet but none quite so gruelling and challenging as Fallujah, in the Al Anbar Governorate of Iraq. This region is often referred to as the toughest and deadliest arena of the entire 2003–11 war in Iraq. The fighting was bloody and the losses significant on both sides of the battle lines. Jason and his fellow American soldiers had a mission to remove the Iraqi insurgents, who included many Al Qaeda fighters.

As the war drew to a close, Jason was excited to reunite with his family and celebrate Halloween with his children. This vision of being with the people he loved the most was a powerful motivator and an intrinsic desire that helped him see out his time in Iraq. Before leaving Iraq, he was sent out one last time on a deadly mission to find one of the most-wanted insurgent leaders. In the darkness of the Iraqi night, Jason and his SEAL team closed in on their target, only to be ambushed and outnumbered by highly effective fighters.

Jason was shot several times in the face, one bullet entering his jaw and coming out at his nose. He found himself pinned to the ground with a blown-out cheekbone, and his medic was shot through the leg. For the next 45 minutes a firefight between Jason's team and the enemy forces went on just a few inches above him. He lost almost half his blood volume and was drifting in and out of consciousness. Each time he came to, he thought, 'Stay awake to stay alive.' He knew that his military medics had such a high rate of success in saving lives that all he had to do was to get through this battle. His motivation to survive and return home to spend those magic moments with his family was deeply embedded in his mind. When most would have given up, Jason persisted. In fact, he called in the closest ever air strike of the Iraq War, essentially asking air support to send in a strike on his own coordinates. He knew that the odds of survival without air support was close to zero, and he was highly motivated to get his team off Iraqi soil and back to base.

Fast forward a number of days, and Jason woke up in Bethesda military hospital in America. He couldn't talk because there was a pipe in his neck helping him to breathe,

Multiply Your Motivation

and he discovered from medical practitioners that he was unlikely to walk again, let alone go to the gym or continue in the SEALs. Can you imagine the devastation he must have felt at that moment?

But Jason's response to adversity is the greatest lesson in human tenacity, resilience and motivation. He grew tired of the sympathy and sorrow directed his way by visitors to his hospital room. He firmly believes that chasing comfort doesn't make us better people. So he had a sign made up for his door, and only those who read it and agreed to it were permitted to go in. His sign read, 'Attention to all who enter here. If you are coming into this room with sorrow or to feel sorry for my wounds, go elsewhere. The wounds I received I got in a job I love, doing it for people I love, supporting the freedom of a country I deeply love. I am incredibly tough and will make a full recovery. What is full? That is the absolute utmost physically my body has the ability to recover. Then I will push that about 20 per cent further through sheer mental tenacity. This room you are about to enter is a room of fun, optimism and intense rapid regrowth. If you are not prepared for that, go elsewhere.'

This powerful sign speaks volumes about Jason's belief in overcoming adversity, his commitment to greatness and his ability to embrace high-performance motivation deeply. That intrinsic drive was enough to equip him with the fuel he needed to recover fully, regaining full use of his limbs and returning to physical fitness. Months later, he was invited to, along with his family, present this sign to the president at the White House. President Bush signed it and it now resides at Bethesda Naval Hospital (now Walter Reed National Medical Center). The Sign on the Door now hangs in the middle of the Wounded Ward and continues to inspire the wounded warriors. Jason's response to adversity is a reminder to all that we can tap into audacious levels of motivation and burning desire. Jason wanted nothing more than to get his troops home and reunite with his most precious loved ones. He now travels the globe sharing his profound lessons.

You're likely not fighting for your life in a firefight right now, but you will undoubtedly face a major ambush in your life in the near future. If you're not facing it right now, it could be just around the corner. These inconvenient and unwelcome surprises are often enough to throw us off course in pursuing our El Capitan. That is, of course, unless we can tap into limitless amounts of intrinsic drive and motivation. Your Altair is deeply meaningful to you, and this world needs you to keep pursuing it with passion. Too many potential high performers give up because they lack the desire, day in, day out over a period of years and decades. But you're going to be different, because you're going to learn what helps the Jason Redmans of the world keep pursuing greatness.

Inside of you burns a fire, and it requires fuel to stay alight. That fuel comes in the form of motivation and desire. Desire is to a result what fuel is to a fire. That's where the term 'burning desire' comes from. It's your responsibility to keep those flames stoked.

Principle 15: Success is an inside job

Not all motivation was created equal. There are two distinct forms of motivation: extrinsic and intrinsic. I prefer to refer to the extrinsic form as motivation and intrinsic form as desire. Extrinsic motivation is defined as a motivation to participate in an activity based on meeting an external goal, garnering praise and approval, winning a competition, or receiving an award or payment. Things like money, fame, cars, houses, clothing, social standing and job title are all examples of extrinsic motivators. People who are largely driven by these rewards are often seeking external validation, and sometimes end up in a constant pursuit of more. In my experience of working with professional athletes and other high performers, people who pursue extrinsic motivation often experience less joy, meaning and fulfilment.

On the other side of the coin, we can all tap into intrinsic motivation – the motivation to engage in a behaviour because of the inherent satisfaction of the activity rather than the desire for a reward or specific outcome. In other words, we do an activity because we enjoy it or we see it as an opportunity to learn and grow. Can you think of a task that you were driven to complete because of how you felt about the task itself, not because you were going to get a reward? Perhaps it's playing a musical instrument because you enjoy it. Or tending your garden, including those weeds! Perhaps it's volunteering for an organisation in your community. Your drive to complete these tasks comes from within. This is desire. Desire is to a result what fuel is to a fire. When you have this built-in desire, you are driven to act. Procrastination and indecision simply don't feature on your mental radar.

In his book *Drive*, author Daniel Pink explores the power of intrinsic motivation and how it fuels high performance. When I spoke to him on my podcast, Daniel shared that traditional rewards like money and status, while effective for simple tasks, are not enough to sustain true, long-term success. 'Obviously, we eat when we're hungry, we drink when we're thirsty, and we know we're motivated by extrinsic things we're rewarded by,' Pink said. 'We're motivated by rewards and punishments in our environment. If you reward behaviour, you get more of it. You punish behaviour, you get less of it. But I think we've neglected that other drive, that intrinsic drive, which is to do things because they matter, because we like them, because we care. And that was, I think, leaving a huge amount of human capacity on the table.'

Intrinsic and extrinsic rewards are each essential for high-performance outcomes. I don't think we'd see billions of people turning up to do their work if zero extrinsic rewards were present. Imagine you managed a team of salespeople and your boss told you that you would no longer be paid from next week onwards. How motivated would you be to spend the next few years working there for free?

Pink shared his views on that too: 'Let me be clear … the idea that people don't care about money or status is nonsense. Of course, they do. And the idea that the only motivator that people want at their job is our intrinsic motivators is also nonsense. You have to pay people well. You have to pay people fairly ... There's a certain kind of extrinsic motivator that psychologists call 'controlling contingent motivators'. I call them, 'if/then rewards'. If you do this, then you get that. If you do this, you'll get promoted. If you do this, you'll get the bonus. What 60 years of research now tells us is that if/then motivators are pretty effective for simple tasks with short time horizons. If you want people to do something that's relatively straightforward and not for that long and they can see the finish line, they're actually really effective.'

Daniel offers up a much more powerful and effective approach to motivation. He emphasises three core elements of intrinsic motivation: autonomy, mastery and purpose. Autonomy gives us the freedom to shape our work; mastery provides the challenge of continuous improvement; and purpose connects our efforts to something larger than ourselves. Success really is an inside job – when you are internally driven by passion, meaning and self-direction, your potential for growth and achievement is significantly enhanced.

Finding positive motivation

It's important to note that both forms of motivation are present the majority of the time. Extrinsic and intrinsic motivation are not additive, they are interactive. So the addition of extrinsic motivators may either diminish or enhance intrinsic motivation.

The following external motivators have been shown to have a negative impact on our intrinsic motivation: monetary rewards, deadlines, threats of punishment, competition against others and negative feedback. You could look at these from a professional standpoint and conclude that giving people financial rewards for meeting strict deadlines is actually going to rewire them to do the work for the wrong reasons, and they'll likely burn out or lose interest at some point. Equally, parents could look at the same list and reconsider their approach to getting their child to behave in a certain way. According to a leading child psychologist, rewards charts, threats of punishment such as going to their room, and timed countdowns are all counterintuitive.

Some external motivators have, however, been shown to have a positive impact on our intrinsic motivation, namely choice, acknowledgement, encouragement towards self-initiation, positive feedback and autonomy. It's so important that we take a moment to understand what drives us and if it comes from within us or from outside of us. Neither is bad, but certainly we want to lean on the side of being motivated from within.

MOTIVATION CHECK-IN
Let's do a quick check-in.

Step 1: Look at what you do
Take out your journal and use a fresh page to list three to five roles or activities you have in your life at the moment. It might be your job, a hobby you enjoy, your parenting

role or something you do for your community. Beside each of them, write down what truly motivates you to do it. Be honest with yourself, and include things like payment, status, contribution and anything else that comes to mind.

Step 2: Analyse your drivers
Have a good look at your list. Now that you have an idea of what motivates you, are you more driven by external or internal factors? If you're driven by a lot of external factors, this is an opportunity to look for intrinsic drivers. If you're serious about playing with a high-performance edge, and taking your life from great to greatest, then desire is going to be a key ingredient.

Step 3: Find your two dominant drivers
Take another look and see if you can rank your drivers from most to least important. Which are your two dominant drivers? Try to be honest with yourself and think about the key elements that really inform your thoughts, behaviours and decisions. When I first did this, I realised that certainty and significance were very prominent drivers in my life. When I analysed that, I realised that I was highly stressed, concerned about what others thought and deeply bored. I knew I needed to change if I was ever to achieve my Altair.

Are you happy with your two dominant drivers or would you like them to change? Keep working through this chapter and you can ensure your drivers are leading you towards your long-term goals.

Principle 16: Master your needs, master your life

There are six core human needs essential for a purposeful life:

1. certainty
2. variety
3. significance
4. love or connection
5. growth
6. contribution

No matter our age, ethnicity, background, gender or race, we all strive to meet these six core human needs. The first four are our basic needs and the last two are our spiritual needs. We must meet the four basic needs in order to devote more of our focus and energy to the last two, which will fill our cup and bring us a sense of meaning.

When we meet all six needs in an empowering way, we experience fulfilment and meaning in our life. If you want to stay in the game long enough to reach the summit of your El Cap, it will become crucial that you strive to meet your needs. Self-doubt, depression, anxiety, self-loathing and hopelessness can often stem from not meeting our core needs.

Let's unpack each one of these needs.

1. Certainty

Certainty is the foundational pillar of our existence. It's the bedrock of comfort, the assurance that our physical needs are met – a safe home, the surety of food, and access to medical care. This need for certainty traverses all life stages, showing up differently in each. It's not just about physical safety, it's about the psychological comfort of predictability and stability in our daily lives.

What constitutes certainty, however, is deeply personal. For some it's the simplicity of a consistent routine and modest living. At its core, certainty is about creating a sense of security and grounding, a protective bubble that allows us to navigate life with confidence.

2. Variety

Variety is proverbially the spice of life, offering unpredictability and the excitement of the unknown. Life thrives on this balance of stability and change. Routine, while comforting, can become boring, prompting a desire for the freshness of new things. For many, the challenges and surprises of life's ups and downs provide this much-needed variety. Variety embodies the elements of change, excitement and the unexpected – all vital for a life lived fully.

3. Significance

The pursuit for significance is a universal human need. It's about feeling valued, necessary and uniquely important. From infancy, where the desire to be the centre of attention prevails, to adulthood, where we strive to carve out our distinct identity, the need for significance shapes much of our journey.

Significance can manifest in various positive ways, driving us to elevate our standards, achieve more and build something meaningful. But when the pursuit of significance becomes an obsession, it can hinder genuine connections with others.

Some people find a sense of importance in ensuring their family's welfare or in work that feels meaningful. Others may find significance in making substantial contributions to society, amassing wealth or even, paradoxically, through the acknowledgment of their struggles and failures.

4. Love and connection

We all need to find love and connection. This deep-seated requirement for meaningful relationships is an essential aspect of our wellbeing. A baby's growth, both physical and emotional, relies heavily on affectionate care, highlighting the importance of these emotional bonds during our lifetime.

As we progress through different life stages, our approach to love and connection takes various shapes. For many, romantic love is central, but cultural differences can shift this focus to love from family, friends and the community.

Love and connection are about belonging, companionship, friendship and affection.

5. Growth

Growth is an indispensable element of humanity; it's what keeps us vibrant and alive. This intrinsic need spans all dimensions of our being – mind, body and soul.

The principle of growth applies universally. If we wish to hold onto something we value – be it wealth, health, relationships or happiness – we need to nurture it so it develops. If we're not growing, we're decaying.

People pursue growth in different ways. Some find that enhancing their physical and mental wellbeing through physical exercise is the path to growth. Others dive into reading and learning, absorbing new ideas and perspectives.

6. Contribution

Contribution reflects our journey beyond personal fulfilment towards positively impacting others. It's about enriching lives, not just our own, but those around us. This sense of contribution is fundamental to feeling complete and content. It's rooted in the human desire to make a difference, to leave a legacy.

Contribution is not just an option; it's essential to feeling satisfaction, contentment and joy.

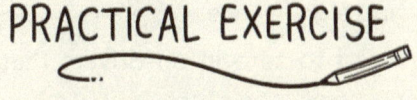

IDENTIFY YOUR FUTURE DRIVERS

Each of us will do certain things, consciously or subconsciously, to meet our core needs. But as we saw in the previous exercise, we often have one or two dominant needs that drive our behaviours. Which two core needs are your dominant drivers in life right now? When I realised that I could shift my dominant need drivers away from certainty and significance, I decided to shift them to growth and connection. It took several years, but making this change has transformed my life in myriad ways. I now have the mindset of 'What can I learn here?' rather than 'I need to know all the answers.'

Open your journal, and draw up a table with two columns. In the left column, write your two current dominant drivers. In the right column, write the two you would like to embrace at your core. This simple exercise will significantly impact your thoughts and decisions, which in turn will dictate your performance in life and work. When you choose your future dominant drivers, ensure that they will help you move towards your Altair while maintaining your values and integrity. For example, if someone is trying to build a billion-dollar company, then being driven by contribution and love will still help them get there. The difference is that they will feel connected and make a genuine difference to other people's lives rather than being driven by certainty and significance.

Take all the time you need to zero in on drivers that truly resonate for you.

To drive it home, let's look at two different characters who met their needs. It's important to note that we all find ways to meet our needs, and those ways can be either empowering or the opposite.

Pick your least favourite dictator from history. No matter who you selected, they will have met their six core human needs in the most disempowering, negative manner possible. They met their need for certainty by exerting power over everybody around them. They met their need for variety by continually invading new countries and territories. They met their need for significance by winning battles and ensuring millions followed their every move. They met their need for connection by murdering innocent people, a deeply disturbing way of connecting with other humans. They met their need for growth by continually expanding their empire. Lastly, they met their need for contribution by convincing themselves they were making the world a better place.

Let's look at a very different example. Mother Teresa, the saint and humanitarian, met her core needs in the opposite way. She met her need for certainty by knowing that she had the ability to help others. She met her need for variety by continually helping different people with different challenges. She met her need for significance by knowing she was making a difference. She met her need for love by serving others. She met her need for growth by continually increasing the number of people she was helping, including starting schools. And finally, she met her need for contribution by being the ultimate servant leader.

The stark contrast between these two humans demonstrates how we always find a way to meet our needs. How you meet your own needs, be they empowering or disempowering, is up to you. Your Altair and El Capitan will inform a lot of your actions, but your values and beliefs will have the biggest influence. If you skimmed over the

> values and beliefs segment of the book, please go back to section one and two, and spend as much time as you need to connect with what you truly believe in. A strong internal compass is what will help you when you most need it. And trust me, when you're scaling a summit like El Cap, you will experience moments of fear, doubt, worry, panic and dread. That compass will ensure you stay the course.

Principle 17: High performance is hormonal

The model of the six core human needs is, in my view, a critical piece of the puzzle that we should all understand. Whether you're a parent, hobbyist, lawyer, athlete or any other driven human, it's essential that you to come to grips with it. If you start to explore the psychology of motivation, you will undoubtedly encounter Maslow's hierarchy of needs, Deci and Ryan's self-determination theory, and goal-setting theory. But it's important to also appreciate that there's a physiological side to motivation. Understanding how dopamine and other neurochemicals operate can give you a powerful tool for optimising your performance.

Motivation can be defined as 'the set of processes through which organisms regulate the probability, proximity and availability of stimuli'. In other words, motivation is how living things (us mere mortals in this instance) control how likely they are to seek out and get close to things that matter to them. Think of it as a system in our body that decides what's important, gives it value and helps us decide what to do about it.

Imagine your brain as a network of different areas working together, connected by pathways of nerves. These areas signal what's important, decide how much we should care about it and help us choose our actions. One important pathway – the mesolimbic dopamine system – connects the midbrain to areas that mediate reward and pleasure, memory, emotions and complex thinking, is vital for motivation. Each area in this pathway has two-way communication with the others and reacts to things that are important or rewarding to us.

Our hormones and motivation

Some of the key players when it comes to motivation are the neurotransmitters dopamine, serotonin, norepinephrine and endorphins. These chemicals are released in response to activities we find rewarding and relay messages between certain parts of the brain that motivate us to seek out these activities again. If you're serious about playing in the rare air of your industry, sport or hobby, then a basic understanding of what's going on inside your body will be a tactical advantage. High performance is hormonal.

Dopamine

Dopamine is often referred to as the reward neurotransmitter. It is released during pleasurable situations and it stimulates us to seek out that enjoyable activity again and again. When we complete something challenging, like a mountain climb or a 5000-piece jigsaw puzzle, the sense of satisfaction we feel is largely due to the release of dopamine. Dopamine motivates us to move forward and act, and a lack of it has the opposite effect. Starving rats with almost no dopamine in their brain lack the motivation to retrieve food even if it's only a few inches away. If we lack that release of dopamine, we're very unlikely to pursue our goals. No matter how great our calendar or accountability coach, we won't have enough juice in our system to pursue our El Cap.

It's important to note that we can overdo the dopamine-fuelling activities too. Too much of a good thing can lead to a dopamine crash, where activities that used to bring us joy now elicit feelings only of numbness. In her book *Dopamine Nation*, US psychiatrist Dr Anna Lembke talks about the balance between pleasure and pain in the brain. Because the brain naturally tries to maintain this balance, if we engage in pleasure-inducing activities too frequently, the brain responds by decreasing dopamine production, leading to feelings of restlessness and dissatisfaction once the remaining dopamine wears off.

This means that high performers must develop the ability to resist short-term rewards in favour of long-term success. Our brains are wired to seek pleasure and avoid pain, but indulging too often in quick dopamine hits (like checking social media or eating junk food) can sabotage our focus and discipline. We can train ourselves to endure discomfort and delay gratification, both of which are critical for staying disciplined and committed to our long-term goals. High performance depends on the ability of an individual, or team, to persist with challenging tasks without giving in to short-term distractions.

Serotonin

Serotonin is a key neurotransmitter in regulating mood, which in turn affects motivation. When we look under the hood, we discover that serotonin is also involved in regulating anxiety, impulsive behaviour and learning. It's worth noting that many medications for depression target serotonin.

Serotonin is linked to motivation through its effects on decision-making, especially when effort is required to achieve rewards. Research shows that lower serotonin levels can diminish our ability or willingness to exert effort for rewards, which are crucial for motivated behaviour.

Serotonin is often associated with mood regulation; when serotonin levels are low, motivation tends to decline. Low serotonin has been connected with the inability to feel pleasure, which directly impacts our drive and motivation to pursue activities or goals that previously brought us joy.

Norepinephrine

Also known as noradrenaline, norepinephrine plays a part in alertness and arousal. Higher levels lead to increased readiness to act, which is essential for motivation. Many of the professional athletes I coach often experience a surge of norepinephrine during games or matches, which helpfully heightens their focus and readiness. In any situation where motivation is driven by potential rewards or the anticipation of positive outcomes, norepinephrine plays a critical role in determining how strongly we will pursue a goal.

Low levels of norepinephrine are often associated with fatigue, difficulty concentrating and low motivation, while elevated levels can make us feel more energetic. Norepinephrine is integral in sustained attention and mental clarity, which give an individual a high-performance edge.

In high-performance arenas such as sport or business, the ability to stay focused under pressure is often the difference between success and mediocrity.

Endorphins

Humanity's natural painkiller, endorphins are produced in the brain and are released during stress or discomfort, helping to alleviate pain while often inducing feelings of euphoria. This can be really helpful in sport or challenging work situations, where pushing through discomfort is absolutely necessary.

The release of endorphins is also part of a reward system in the brain, reinforcing positive behaviour and increasing the desire to continue with an activity. Knowing that a reward of feeling good will follow motivates high performers to engage more intently in physical or mental tasks. As high performers, we need to sustain our focus and drive over long periods if we are to achieve our long-term goals. Having endorphins do their thing will help us significantly.

Hungarian-American psychologist Mihaly Csikszentmihalyi dedicated many years of his life to understanding the flow state – that beautiful situation where we are so deeply focused on a single task that time seems to fly by. The good news is that endorphins contribute to our ability to enter a flow state. To increase your connection with your chosen endeavour and to avoid distractions, tapping into this powerful neurotransmitter will be crucial.

As an added bonus, endorphins play a role in reducing stress, particularly through exercise. They help regulate mood and emotional responses. The release of beta-endorphins during exercise, for example, is associated with a euphoric state and pain reduction, which contributes to stress relief. This is often referred to as a runner's high. Several studies have shown that the release of endorphins during exercise may also provide long-term mental health benefits, helping reduce anxiety and improve emotional resilience. This shows that regular exercise is a vital strategy for high-performers in moving towards their short- and long-term goals.

Harnessing our hormones

It's all very well knowing more about the hormones behind our motivation, but how do we actually have an influence on them? Here's how.

Sleep

How much sleep we get directly affects our levels of several hormones such as the stress hormone cortisol, the hunger hormone leptin and growth hormone, which is involved in brain function, healthy muscle retention and fat metabolism. There are numerous devices that can help us monitor our sleep. For some time now I've been wearing an Oura ring, which provides me with data and insights regarding my sleep.

This has allowed me to influence my sleep in a positive way. Some simple ways of improving your sleep include:

- Doing an early-morning workout, or even taking a brisk walk. This will supercharge your levels of the hormone melatonin and boost the effects of natural sleep.
- Not having screens in the bedroom. The blue light emitted negatively affects melatonin levels, making it harder to fall asleep.
- Eliminating coffee 12 hours before bedtime. Caffeine has a quarter-life of 12 hours, which means that if you enjoy a coffee at 9 am, about 25 per cent of that caffeine will still be present in your system at 9 pm.
- Adopting the 3-2-1 approach. Three hours before bed, stop working; two hours before bed, stop eating and drinking; and one hour before bed, switch off all screens. This evening ritual will signal to your body and mind that it's time to down-regulate and prepare for sleep.
- Breathing. Simply breathing intentionally before bed will help reduce stress and increase relaxation. Try a simple two-minute breathing exercise where you inhale through the nose for six counts, and exhale slowly for eight counts. The increased exhalation will help to reduce your heart rate and create a sense of relaxation.

Diet

Our nutritional intake can significantly affect our levels of neurotransmitters. Foods rich in tryptophan (such as whole grains, legumes, nuts and dairy) increase serotonin levels, while tyrosine-rich foods (such as soybeans, sesame seeds, nuts and meat) boost dopamine production.

Movement

As we've already seen, moving our body is a potent stimulator of endorphin release and also enhances dopamine and serotonin levels, directly impacting out mood and motivation. The more regularly we exercise, the more self-determined we are.

Exercise is also a vital component of longevity, which we need if we're to stay in the game long enough to realise our full potential. A longitudinal study in America that followed 116,221 adults over a 30-year period assessed the impact of leisure-time physical activity on mortality risk.

These key takeaways from the study might inspire you to continue your commitment to exercise:

- Engaging in vigorous physical activity two to four times longer than the minimum recommendations of 2.5–5 hours a week significantly lowered the risk of death from cardiovascular diseases.
- Those who exercised two to four times longer than moderate activity guidelines (5–10 hours a week) enjoyed the greatest benefits.
- Participants who engaged in two to four times longer than moderate activity guidelines experienced a 26–31 per cent reduction in overall mortality and had a 28–38 per cent lower risk of dying from cardiovascular diseases.

Stress management through mindfulness

Chronic stress can deplete neurotransmitters like serotonin and dopamine, leading to decreased motivation. However, techniques such as mindfulness and meditation can help maintain optimal levels. Psychological research has shown that people who receive mindfulness therapy are less likely to react to stress with negative thoughts or disempowering emotions.

It's important to note that stress is psychological. Events don't cause stress. What causes stress are the views we take of events around us. The more mindful we are, the more potential views we have and the less stressed, and thus healthier, we're likely to be.

I was fortunate enough to sit down with the Mother of Mindfulness, Dr Ellen Langer. She's a globally renowned psychologist and professor at Harvard University. Here's what she shared with me about mindfulness: 'People confuse it with meditation, and meditation started in the East. Meditation is a wonderful practice. It has nothing to do with mindfulness per se; you meditate to result in post-meditative mindfulness. Mindfulness, as we study it, isn't a practice. It's actually a way of being that's derived from two things: either a top-down approach recognising we don't know anything ... or a bottom-up approach, by actively noticing things you think you know.' In essence, mindfulness is about heightening awareness.

Dr Langer and her colleague Alia Crum conducted a study with hotel chambermaids who didn't believe their physically demanding work counted as exercise. They divided the participants into two groups, and told one group that their daily tasks were equivalent to exercise. Without any other lifestyle changes, the group who viewed their work as exercise showed measurable health improvements. 'The people who just changed their minds and now saw their work as exercise lost weight,' Ellen told me. 'There was a change in body mass index, waist-to-hip ratio, and their blood pressure came down.' The women in the other group did not change. The chambermaid study highlights how simply shifting our perception of everyday activities – being mindful of how these activities are beneficial – can lead to measurable physical health improvements. This study exemplifies how mindfulness, in the form of active awareness and noticing, can have a profound impact on both mental and physical wellbeing.

After my conversation with Dr Langer, I decided to note the key action points arising from it so that I could become more mindful. Here's how you can embrace it too:

1. **Recognise uncertainty**: Acknowledge that you don't know everything. By embracing the fact that things look different from different perspectives and are always changing, you'll pay closer attention to the world around you. In Ellen's words, 'If you fully appreciate that you don't know, you pay attention to everything.'
2. **Actively notice differences**: Instead of relying on assumptions or automatic responses, actively notice variations in things you think you already know. As my wise mentor reminds me often, 'Assumptions are the mother of all faux pas.' This active noticing could be

something as simple as observing how the colour of leaves changes at different times of the year or noticing how your feelings fluctuate.

3. **Be present and aware:** Mindfulness is a way of being that involves bringing attention to the present moment and recognising the opportunities and choices that are available to us when we're aware of our surroundings and thoughts. As Langer told me, 'When you're mindful, all of a sudden you have choices that you weren't aware were there.'

Over the years, I've experienced stress related to work, finances, earthquakes, relationships and several other factors. I've built a regular meditation and breathwork practice into my daily routine that has significantly lowered my stress, heart rate and emotional reactivity. I was certainly a lot more vocally reactive in my twenties before embracing Eastern practices. It takes time to integrate these sorts of techniques, but with patience and consistency you will add a very powerful tool to your psychosomatic toolkit.

MEDITATION

There are so many different forms of meditation, and I am by no means an expert, but I have practised a very simple technique that has served me powerfully. You can give it a whirl too.

You need to know something critically important about meditation first, though. Meditation is *not* about clearing your mind and having no thoughts. If anyone tells you that's what meditation is, run a mile. The human mind does not function in a way that allows us to just clear away every thought.

I believe meditation is the ability to focus on a single point and become aware of your distracting thoughts. And when you realise that a random thought has floated in, it's about going back to the single focal point gently and persistently. For me, meditation is building the muscle of focus. To build our focusing ability, we must learn to focus on one single point.

Breathing meditation

Here's the simple meditation technique I use. Set an alarm for two minutes. Sit or lie down and close your eyes. Breathe normally and focus on your belly moving in and out or up and down, or focus on the air moving in and out of your nose or mouth. Each time you find yourself thinking of other things, go gently back to focusing on your breathing. Continue to do this until your alarm goes off. Practise this twice daily – morning and evening is my preference – for a few weeks, then start to increase it by a few minutes each week until you are up to 10 or 15 minutes. If you prefer to keep your eyes open, then simply light a candle and focus on the flame instead of your breath.

I'll let you in on a secret. About ten minutes before I go on stage to deliver an address, I always find my heart rate elevated. It can often be as much as 110–120 beats per minute. I usually find a bathroom and practise this simple breathing meditation, which brings my heart rate down below 100 bpm within a minute or two. Meditation doesn't need to involve the lotus position and burning incense – it can be very pragmatic. I see it as a high-performance tool, one that we can leverage to our advantage.

Make a commitment to try meditation for at least the next week. Note down in your journal the benefits you feel, then go for a month. Soon it will become a habit you will make time for on the busiest of days.

Principle 18: Clarity precedes action

You are now better equipped than 99 per cent of the global population to deeply understand what drives you to do the things you do. Understanding motivation and desire is a crucial component of high performance and of winning. Where to from here? It's time to consolidate what you've learned. Unless you're keen on a mediocre outcome, remember that clarity precedes action. If at this point you still feel doubt about your goals and what drives you to achieve them, go back and work through everything again. Before you pack your bags for your El Capitan expedition, take the time to get clear on what motivates you and how you can influence your biology and psychology.

To reinforce how critical it is to get radically clear, let me share the example of Scott 'Razor' Robertson. Razor is a highly respected New Zealand rugby coach and former All Black. As head coach of the Crusaders, one of the most successful teams in the Super Rugby championship, he led his team to win seven Super Rugby titles from 2017 to 2023. This remarkable achievement solidified his reputation as one of the most successful coaches in rugby history.

Razor shared with me how clarity of vision was crucial for his success with the Crusaders. When he first joined the team in 2017, the Crusaders hadn't won a championship in nine years. Scott was able to instil a clear vision for the team, inspired by Muhammad Ali's 'Rumble in the Jungle' fight. He's a huge fan of having a theme that everyone can connect to and embrace. He adapted this story to create a powerful metaphor for the team, framing their journey as one of resilience and strategy, much like Ali's comeback against George Foreman.

He didn't just stop at a metaphor; he brought clarity to every aspect of the team's language and behaviour. He changed their vernacular, using aggressive words like *jab*, *punch* and *hook* for defence, helping the players embody this mindset on the field. This clear and cohesive vision allowed the team to rally around a purpose, and ultimately win the 2017 final in a landmark victory.

Razor has developed a masterful skill of providing a clear and emotionally compelling vision that helps his team understand their mission and execute it with precision and passion. 'I love to tell a story, to bring a vision alive so people can see it,' he told me. 'I put it in their head, and then we go and get it.' In everything he does as one of the world's greatest coaches, it's clear that he embraces the principle that clarity precedes action.

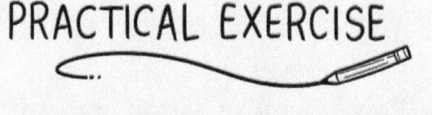 

SUPERCHARGE YOUR MOTIVATION

Now it's your turn to supercharge your motivation to go after your dreams, goals and aspirations.

Step 1: Zoom in on your motivators

Grab your journal and answer the following:

- **What two dominant drivers am I going to focus on?**
  Write down the two core human drivers that you know will help you live a deeply meaningful life while pursuing your El Cap. You will have identified these drivers earlier in this chapter.
- **What are my intrinsic motivators for chasing down my El Cap?**
  Write down the reasons you're motivated to take big action. These are the motivators that don't include external factors such as money, fame or status.
- **What are two lifestyle factors I must embrace?**
  Write down two habits you will implement to increase your ability to focus and stay motivated. These can be related to sleep, diet, exercise or stress management.

> **Step 2: Keep up the motivation**
> Make sure you remind yourself regularly of your key drivers and your intrinsic motivators. In Chapter 6 you will learn how to successfully implement the two new lifestyle habits you have chosen.

Desire is to a result what fuel is to a fire – you have to want success to achieve it. You're here on earth with a gift and a mission. This world is relying on you to share your innate genius – your gifts and greatness. Sadly, too few realise their potential because they lack the desire to stay in the long game. To ensure you develop a deep intrinsic drive to pursue your passionate purpose, harness every possible insight and tool available to you. The rare air awaits you, and the world will rejoice when you step up to the plate to be your greatest self. Being a one-percenter is not easy, yet meandering through life along with the masses is equally difficult. Both can be painful, but one path produces meaning while the other cultivates regret.

There's one behaviour you can develop today that will shape memorable tomorrows: simply get out of your head and onto the page. It's the one habit that many of the billionaires and movement makers I've coached and interviewed all embrace. Be a one-percenter; tread the path less trodden. Keep your journal close at hand and make an effort to explore your desire and motivation regularly. Where your focus goes, your energy follows.

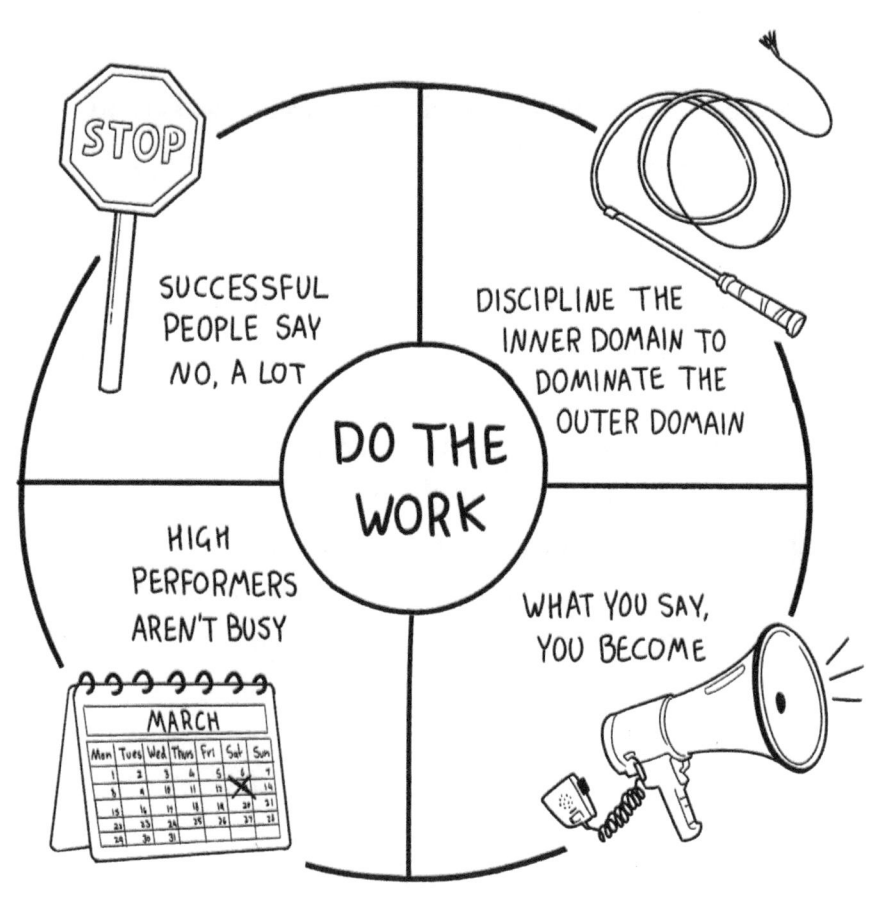

5

DO THE WORK

Congrats on making it this far. Honestly. Most people buy a book, read a chapter or two and then resign it to shelf-help (those self-help books that populate the shelf rather than the mind). You've done the heavy lifting already, which says a lot about your personal discipline. The things we'll be covering in this chapter are usually where most people begin. They jump right into the doing, the grafting, the habits and the discipline required to be world-class at their craft. But it's useful to remember what we learned earlier: common sense isn't always common practice.

In this case, the commonsense approach would be to get clear on where you're headed, why you want it so badly and what drivers you'll need to get there – before hitting the road. Most people neglect the deep work, partly because it's difficult and partly because they lack the discipline to focus. When you learn to distil your focus, you set yourself apart from the crowd. The masses are magnificent at diluting their most precious resource. If only they knew that their El Capitan was 15 centimetres away, maybe they'd develop the discipline to double down on their focus. That's right, 15 centimetres. The 15 centimetres between your two ears is the most valuable real estate you own. It's up to you whether you're going to be a world-class homeowner or a mediocre property manager.

By the end of this chapter you will have a deeper understanding of how to develop better discipline, how to supercharge your vernacular, how to multiply your time and how to be a boundary boss. If you've done all the mental and emotional gym work from the last two chapters, you'll find this chapter less intense.

By the end of this chapter you will have developed the tools you need to do the work as only a high performer can, by working through the following principles:

19. Discipline the inner domain to dominate the outer domain.
20. What you say, you become.
21. High performers aren't busy.
22. Successful people say no, a lot.

Principle 19: Discipline the inner domain to dominate the outer domain

Discipline isn't for the faint of heart. It's a commitment – to yourself – to hold yourself to higher standards in many areas of your life. It's a non-negotiable promise in the pursuit of your personal El Cap.

One person springs to mind when I think of self-discipline: long-distance runner Dean Karnazes. He's the ultimate high performer, known as the Ultramarathon Man. Some might know him for his bestselling books, but most know him for the power of his mental discipline to overcome physical limitations. He ran 50 marathons in 50 states over 50 consecutive days. He completed 350 continuous miles (560 kilometres) without sleep. His journey is not just about physical endurance but also about mastering the mind. Along his path, Dean struggled with immense physical pain – like being unable to place his feet on the floor before marathon 19 – and moments of self-doubt when the magnitude of his challenge threatened to overwhelm him. But through sheer discipline, he trained his mind to focus on the present moment, breaking the monumental task into manageable steps. By embracing adversity and removing mental distractions, he pushed further than he ever thought possible. His story underlines the fact that success is built incrementally and requires us to master the inner domain of our mind in order to overcome our outer challenges.

Through chatting to Dean about his high-performance habits on my podcast, I identified four key techniques that he harnessed to discipline his inner domain:

1. **Focusing on the present moment**: Dean mentioned that during difficult moments, such as when his body

was in intense pain, he disciplined his mind to focus on the present. He broke down challenges into smaller, manageable tasks – just focusing on taking the next step. 'I tried my best to be in the here and now,' he told me. 'I said, "Just get to the sink, splash water in your face ... take a step, when the gun goes off, take another step."' No matter how daunting the task at hand might seem, simply focus on the most important next step.

2. **Incremental perseverance**: Dean took an incremental approach to discipline that allowed him to conquer seemingly impossible feats, like running 50 marathons in 50 states. His commitment to being the best version of himself every day showcases the importance of small, disciplined steps in achieving big results. Dean put it perfectly when we explored his story on the show: 'Great things don't happen at once, they happen over time, they accumulate. Fifty days of a marathon proved to me that ... if you have that stick-to-it-ness, if you have the same commitment just to be the best that you can, give it your all, you can achieve greatness.' Committing to the long game is a crucial part of becoming a high performer. Short-game playing leads to short-game results.

3. **Overcoming limitations**: 'Running is about breaking down limitations ... I thought, "If I can do this, I'll prove to myself that really nothing is impossible, and these lessons would carry over from running into

life."' Dean didn't like comparing himself to others but focused on pushing beyond what he thought was possible. He stayed curious in order to fuel his internal drive, revealing that self-discipline often leads to surprising new levels of ability.
4. **Using mental tactics in adversity**: When facing extreme adversity, like the debilitating pain on marathon 19, Dean shared that thinking too much was the problem, so he shifted his focus to being in the present, taking one step at a time. 'When things get really, really tough ... I turned very much inward and just focused on the here and now ... Just take your next step to the best of your ability.'

My challenge to you: Can you visualise the repetitions, the hard yards, the sacrifices? This is exactly what it will take if you want to summit your El Capitan. I wrote this book for the person who is willing to take the big swing. Climbing your local rolling hill is more of a putt. When you commit to ascending your El Capitan, you're committing the next few decades of your life to it. I'm not saying that you won't have time to connect with loved ones or enjoy fun adventures – the opposite, in fact. But you will face many moments when you want to give up on meteoric and settle for mediocre.

If you're truly committed to being the best in your field, then starting to discipline your inner domain is non-negotiable.

Principle 20: What you say, you become

Every single day, we are saying things to others and to ourselves. We often think carefully about the words we use when talking to others, perhaps due to our awareness of how we might make them feel. But we don't spend a lot of time thinking about the words we say to ourselves. Self-talk significantly influences our discipline and performance. While negative self-talk has a disempowering impact on our discipline and motivation, positive self-talk is a vital tool in the high performer's arsenal. Positive self-talk can enhance focus, confidence and perseverance. Studies have even shown that it serves as an effective internal motivator during training and competitive scenarios.

One of the most elite forces on the planet is the US Navy SEALs. Over the years, I've been fortunate enough to connect with a number of former SEALs, all of whom shared with me some of the inspiring, and gory, details of their training and deployment. To become a SEAL, one must complete BUD/S (Basic Underwater Demolition/SEAL) training, which is arguably one of the most gruelling physical and mental challenges known to humankind. One of the weeks is known as Hell Week and the success rate is just 25 per cent. The US Navy decided to bring in a psychologist to address the high failure rates in the intense underwater competency tests. The analysis of the enlisted revealed a pattern of four critical psychological tools being used by the majority of successful trainees. These techniques are designed to enhance mental toughness under pressure:

1. goal setting
2. staying calm
3. mental rehearsal
4. self-talk.

So far in this book you've covered big-picture goal setting with your Altair and El Capitan. You've developed skills to manage your emotions and hormones. You've learned about the power of visualisation. Now we're going to supercharge your self-talk. Exquisite language leads to sublime results.

The power of positive self-talk

Jim Carrey is one of Hollywood's all-time greats, but his beginnings were humble. He had a 9th Grade education and used to work in factories. But all the while he believed that things could change: 'It's a series of crushing disappointments and I just go into a different gear – I go into "don't know how it's gonna write itself, but it will".' He famously shared in an interview with Oprah Winfrey that he wrote a $10 million cheque to himself: 'I wrote myself the check for acting services rendered, and I gave myself five years.' And right before Thanksgiving 1995, he found out that he was going to make $10 million on *Dumb and Dumber*. Jim is a stunning example of focusing on what we want to bring into existence by speaking it and writing it. Where your focus goes, your energy flows, or as Carrey explained, 'Whenever I wanted something to happen, I manifested it.'

What is it that you want to bring into your life? What is the El Cap that will bring you deep meaning and purpose? As a young lad I dreamed of being crowned world juvenile solo drumming champion. I visualised it, I wrote about it and I spoke aloud to myself about the outcome being a reality. I used to sit in my practice room and repeat the incantations, 'I am confident, I am deserving and I am fully committed to being the world's best drummer.' This gave me the motivation to do the work I needed to achieve my dream. Standing on stage in Scotland, receiving the championship gold medal at the age of 13, reinforced to me that the words we tell ourselves have a significant impact on our goals and dreams.

A young professional rugby player once came to me with a concern that he might never make the All Blacks. I asked him what it meant to become an All Black and why it was so important to him. I recommended that he write out a short statement he could say aloud each day, with conviction, in his own private space. This statement reinforced that he was grateful to be an All Black and that he was deserving of the honour. Just 14 months later, he was called to the black jersey. Goosebump moments like that make me so grateful that I can bear witness to great humans striving for mastery. What is your ultimate goal, and are you bringing it to life daily through the spoken word?

A few years ago I was invited to deliver a mental skills session to a renowned professional sports team. They wanted to tap into a competitive edge that would help them when they needed it most. After some time, I discovered that their language had room for refinement. The things they said to themselves personally and collectively were not always driving positive outcomes or behaviours. I sat with the entire group one morning and asked them what was most important to them for the season. We then refined it down to one of their team standards: being relentless. I shared some of my observations about their negative self-talk or when they looked miserable after a dropped ball or non-selection.

One of the players volunteered to join me at the front of the room to try an exercise. The challenge was simply for him to say 'I am relentless.' At first he was quiet, soft and uninspiring. I explained that he shouldn't be saying it just to say it, that he should be saying it to convince not me or his coaches, but his subconscious mind. Our mind can sense incongruence and self-doubt like a shark can detect blood. When we try to deceive our mind, it never loses. It always knows we're lying and trying to trick it. And in return, it will continue to hold us to the standard we accept. Within a few moments, this player was incanting 'I am relentless' with such passion and belief that his own mind was convinced and he received rapturous applause from his teammates.

After this session, the whole team repeated this incantation daily, which had a powerful impact on their motivation, belief and discipline. Once the whole team started to believe they *were* relentless, their fortunes began to change.

When it comes to achieving the impossible, self-talk has to be at the centre of the picture. What you say, you become. Self-talk is the seed of self-mastery.

Self-talk: Can you or can't you?

We have two options with our self-talk:

1. **InCAN'Tations:** I can't, I'm too old, I'm too slow, I'm too tired, I'm broke, I'm too late, I can't hold the ball, I can't win the cup.
2. **InCANtations:** I can take action, I am enough, I am relentless, I can win, I am abundant, I am resourceful.

The choice is yours. And just know that right now, in this very moment, you're saying words to yourself. Have a listen. Are they lifting you up or holding you back?

It baffles me when someone says 'Break a leg' when they're wishing someone good luck for a performance; 'That was so sick' when complimenting someone on a job well done. Or 'She's dope' when it comes to describing someone's personality; 'That's crazy' when someone wins the grand prize. All these words have negative connotations. Although you and I understand at a conscious level that people are trying to make a positive remark, our subconscious mind will connect it with negativity. When this compounds several times (sometimes hundreds of times) each day, it has an impact on our discipline and motivation.

Your perception shapes your reality, and the words you use determine your perception. When you allow negative words and concepts into your thoughts, you are increasing the activity in your brain's fear centre, the amygdala. This in turn triggers the release of hormones such as cortisol, which then flow throughout your system. In short, words carry emotional charges that can influence your perception of reality, your physical states and your overall wellbeing. Words can literally shape and change your brain's structure. Negative words can trigger your brain's defence mechanisms, leading to stress and anxiety, while positive words can increase feelings of motivation and happiness by triggering the release of serotonin and dopamine.

The idea of using affirmations or inCANtations is a way of priming your mind and taking advantage of the brain's ability to reorganise itself by forming new neural connections – known as neuroplasticity. Priming involves exposure to one stimulus in order to influence our response to another stimulus without conscious guidance. The repeated use of certain words can prime our brain to respond in specific ways, reinforcing neural pathways associated with the emotional charges of those words.

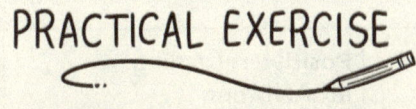 

PRACTICAL EXERCISE

MASTERING INCANTATIONS

You will never scale the heights of your El Cap if you bring yourself down with negative self-talk. Mastering inCANtations will allow you to stay the dizzying climb to the top.

I don't want you to waste valuable time going down the wrong path. If you're going to supercharge your self-talk, make sure you do it with meaning and conviction. Start today. What you say, you become.

High performers always make time to do the work.

Step 1: Listen to your self-talk

I want you to become attuned to the words you're saying to yourself most often. Simply listen out for them over the next 24 hours, then write them down in your journal. Unless you're superhuman, you'll find you've written a number of disempowering words or sentences.

Step 2: Flip your negatives to positives

Now examine some of your less-than-optimal self-talk and flip each one into a positive and empowering version. Ideally, your inCANtations should be guiding stars to aim for in moments of doubt, fear or worry. They should help you move towards your short-term goals and your longer-term El Capitan.

Here are a few examples:

Negative self-talk: InCAN'Tation	Positive reframing: InCANtation
I'm too old.	I'm right where I should be.
I am tired.	I am relentless.
I am weak.	I am strong.
I'm too busy.	I am laser-focused.

Draw up a table like this in your journal and reframe each negative inCAN'Tation.

Step 3: Repeat your inCANtations daily, and with conviction

Writing the words down is only the beginning, but learning to embody and embrace them is a whole other thing. I want you to repeat these incantations daily so that you can start to rewire your beliefs and amplify your discipline. *How* you say the words is critically important, so please ensure you say them with conviction and passion. Your subconscious mind knows when you lack belief in what you're saying. The best time to rehearse your self-talk is in the morning, perhaps in the shower, perhaps on a drive to work or when you're out for a walk.

Principle 21: High performers aren't busy

Are you busy being busy? A client came to me a few years ago and told me how frustrated he was at his lack of results on the work front. He simply wasn't hitting his financial targets, not even close. I became curious.

'Gareth, what's holding you back from hitting your targets and moving towards your El Cap?' I asked.

His response: 'I'm just so busy. In fact I'm too busy.'

'So what I'm hearing is that you don't have the time to execute the behaviours that will help your business and revenue grow. Am I right?'

He looked at me blankly and nodded in agreement.

What happened next made him very uncomfortable. But let's face it, effective coaching shouldn't make the client or performer comfortable. Growth happens when you're in your zone of discomfort. Before I share with you what unfolded, I need you to ask yourself if you ever catch yourself saying, 'I'm busy', 'The week is looking really busy' or 'I'm too busy to [insert healthy empowering habit]'. If you catch those words coming out of your mouth, I have news for you. You're not busy, you simply lack priorities. Do I know your exact circumstance? No. But I have seen hundreds of other people with the same 'busy' problem and taken a look under the hood to uncover the truth.

Here's what I asked Gareth to do: 'Please, get your phone out, go to your calendar and identify where you spent your time during the past week.' After checking his calendar, Gareth shared that he clearly spent a lot of time having coffee or beers with potential clients, as well as business development on the golf course.

We took a moment to analyse the last few months of time spent on these activities and realised that only a small number of them were leading to income generation. The rest of the time, he was frittering away valuable time that he could be using to serve his existing clients or take care of important compliance and administration.

Gareth is not an outlier. Many of us spend time doing things that don't generate the results we desire. Some of us spend too much time socialising, others spend too much time scrolling social media, while others plant themselves on the couch to binge-watch television shows. In fact, one study from the US National Bureau of Economic Research delved into the impact of digital media on mental health and how digital addiction is influenced by psychological factors such as social comparison and the need for gratification. It suggested that digital platforms that cater to these psychological needs reinforce addictive behaviours. The complex relationship between these factors highlights the importance of understanding the psychological mechanisms behind digital addiction in the development of effective interventions. But the good news: the study also highlighted the effectiveness of self-imposed screen-time limits, which suggests that users have some awareness of their addiction but underestimate its extent. The research concluded that self-control issues account for a significant portion of social media usage.

Check your screen time
You have the agency to make a difference to this highly addictive behaviour by simply setting yourself screen-time limits. It's so simple that you can do it using the settings on your phone. Look around you the next time you go to the supermarket, visit a cafe, drive by a bus stop. I promise you, you'll be shocked by how many human heads are peering downward, glued to their phones. I remember a woman in Vancouver, Canada, sharing with me that she was in the habit of normally 'catching up on messages and emails' while she was at her young child's ice hockey games.

One particular day was different. She challenged herself to leave her phone in the car and count how many times her daughter looked up to see if she was watching her. Her seven-year-old looked up a total of 17 times in the first 30 minutes. Imagine how her child felt each week when she saw her mum scrolling on social media instead of showing some interest in her game. Many parents justify this sort of behaviour by saying, 'But I was there. I was at the game.' But were they? Being present requires presence. And presence is the sibling of focus. This Canadian mother looked around at the 12 other parents on the sidelines, and 11 of them were hooked to their phones.

Monotasking beats multitasking, every time

I can't stress enough just how important it is to be present in the moment. When you're trying to do more than one thing, you're essentially attempting to multitask. But our brains are designed to be mono-taskers. And yes, that counts for everyone. Women aren't better at multitasking. The truth is that no one is good at it. Multitasking is something that humans simply aren't capable of. When we attempt it, we mess with our brain's working memory.

The very term 'multitask' originally appeared in 1965 in an IBM paper discussing the capabilities of the IBM System/360. For some reason, we humans decided that we could also function like machines and do two things at once. What we actually do, however, is 'task-switch'. We quickly shift our attention and focus from one task to another while convincing ourselves that we're juggling two tasks simultaneously.

But there are cognitive costs associated with multitasking: task-switching leads to decreased performance accuracy and speed. If you want to make more mistakes and get less done in the same amount of time, then continue with multitasking. Heavy media multitaskers, those who have many media channels open at once and switch between them, have lower working memory performance, which leads to poorer long-term memory performance. There's clearly a neurological concern related to being distracted by your phone, or any screen for that matter.

How would you feel if I said you had only three days to complete a task that you know takes five full days? Or worse, how would you feel if I said you had 34 fewer years on this planet than the average human lifespan? I imagine you'd be unimpressed. But even brief mental blocks created by task-switching can cost as much as 40 per cent of someone's productive time. Being intentional with where you place your focus will have a direct impact on the quality of your work, relationships and health. But there's an emotional concern too.

I was chatting with one of the world's most renowned cricket stars several years ago. We got talking about parenthood, and how challenging it can be to juggle a high-performance career with trying to be a present parent. He told me the following story.

'I was arguably the most successful and prominent cricket star globally at the time. I spent so much time on the road, and I'd usually only be home between 20 and 30 days in a year. I recall a moment standing in my kitchen at home with my young baby in my arms. As my wife prepared dinner, I looked into my daughter's eyes. As I stared into her eyes, all I could think of was the next cricket match. In that moment I felt deeply guilty and shameful. This wake-up call sent me to my mental skills coach, who shared a simple yet powerful approach. He said, "Be where your feet are." It was such a powerful statement and reminded me to be mentally and emotionally present in every moment. From then on, I simply looked down at my feet when I found my mind wandering and said, "Be where your feet are." It was a game-changing mental model for me at this critical point in my career and fatherhood.'

This shared experience really forced me to sit up and realise that presence is the ultimate superpower. If you're keen to perform above the norm, commit to being a mono-tasker. One thing at a time. One singular focus. Radically focus on distilling your focus down to the one thing that will move the needle.

BE PRESENT

Knowing what your priorities are and then behaving in alignment with them is the ultimate success. You have already identified your values and priorities, so now it's about asking yourself if you're building each day around those priorities. If your days don't reflect your priorities, then you're most certainly on a road to being busy being busy, feeling regret and lacking fulfilment. Never forget that your days are your life in miniature.

Here is my challenge to you:

Step 1: Cut your screen time
Set yourself screen-time limits on your device. Choose a duration of time each day that you're happy to spend on specific apps (including email, messages and social media) then stick to it. You will get so much life back. This is the wealth money can't buy.

Step 2: When you're at home, be at home
Before walking through the front door after work each day, take five minutes to clear any emails, messages or calls that you need to deal with. Then pop your phone on flight mode and place it in a drawer out of sight. Spend your evening deep in connection. If you're serious about embracing the self-discipline required to win the long game, then this is non-negotiable.

You can't be a high performer if your mind is digitally diluted. Be a one-percenter and choose to create deep focus with your loved ones, friends, pets and community.

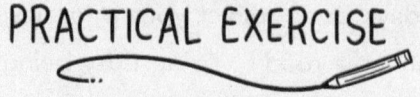

PRACTICAL EXERCISE

THE HIGH-PERFORMANCE TRIAD FOR OPTIMAL PERFORMANCE

My billion-dollar CEO clients and performers who dominate the rare air in their industries all share the same challenges we do. They get busy being busy, but they want to get radically focused to ensure they perform consistently above the standard norms while maintaining healthy relationships and wellbeing.

I teach them a simple but effective technique called the high-performance triad. It will help you get monomaniacal with your priorities. As a youngster striving to become the world's best junior drummer, I was lucky enough to have a teacher write this model out for me.

When do you want to use this framework? Anytime you're feeling stuck, fed up, exhausted, lost, confused, stressed, anxious or busy.

First things first. Purpose is the basis of the entire model. Luckily, you've already identified your purpose – your Altair – but if you skimmed over that part, please go back and do the work. If you want the results, shortcuts aren't an option. This isn't woo-woo affirmations and manifestation, this is truly getting clear on what you really want and getting after it with a powerful, pragmatic process.

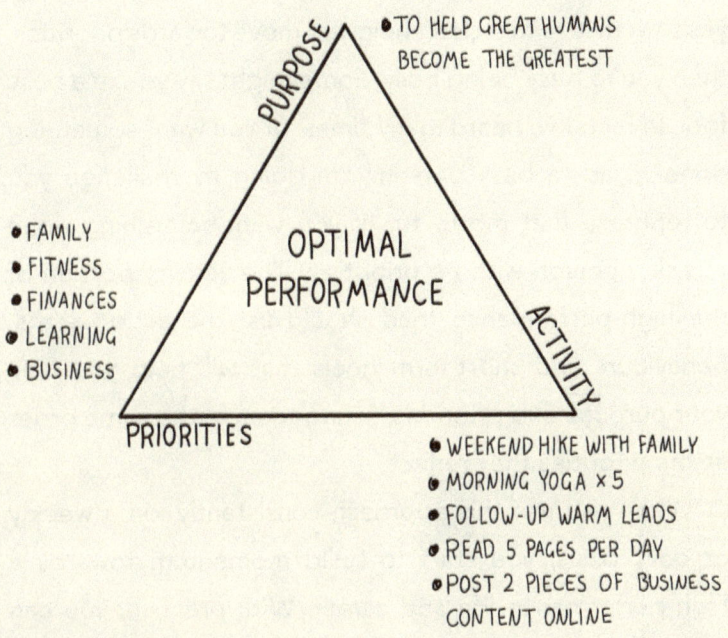

Step 1: Purpose
Take a fresh page in your journal and draw a large triangle. Write your purpose at the top of the triangle.

Step 2: Priorities
Your purpose should shape your priorities. You identified your non-negotiable priorities in Principle 4. Write them down – there should be no more than five. Any more, and you have a to-do list. When you dilute your priorities, you dilute your results.

Step 3: Activity
Lastly, your activity should reflect your priorities. In fact, your priorities should inform your activity. When you say

yes to activities that don't help you move towards priorities, then you're busy being busy. Some might say you're a busy fool. In fact, I've heard many times: 'If you want something done ... ask a busy person.' I'm going to challenge you to rephrase that motto to, 'If you want something done ... ask a person with no priorities.' The activity portion of the high-performance triad should list the action steps, behaviours and short-term goals that will help you fulfil your purpose and priorities, listing them in the same order as the priorities they reflect.

When you use this approach consistently, on a weekly or daily basis, you start to build momentum towards a high-performance life and career. With practice, you can become more efficient at prioritising tasks, which will improve your ability to manage them effectively. This will lead to enhanced performance and cognitive flexibility, which will enable you to adapt more effectively to changing demands and environments. And this ability to adapt can lead to superior decision-making and problem-solving skills, which will contribute to your overall personal and professional growth. It's a powerful chain of consequence.

Principle 22: Successful people say no, a lot

When Scott O'Neil was the CEO of Harris Blitzer Sports & Entertainment (HBSE), he built it from a company managing a single team, the Philadelphia 76ers NBA team (aka the Sixers), into a huge sports and entertainment franchise with two professional sports teams and an e-sports business. When he was in charge, the Sixers signed the first jersey sponsorship agreement in the history of the sport. He was later the CEO of Madison Square Garden, New York, managing the venue and its associated entertainment company.

During his time at the helm, he was recognised for creating an innovative and best-in-class workplace and workforce, and the Sixers were named one of the Top 50 Cultures in the USA by *Entrepreneur* magazine. Scott was personally named Most Innovative Executive and the Sixers were awarded five Clio awards, including one for Team of the Year in 2021.

In summary, Scott would have been regarded by most as a high performer – someone who was successful in his career. But I got to know Scott over the years, and was able to go a little deeper with him on my podcast. In our conversations he was so open and honest, sharing his struggles with finding the right balance and doing 80–100-hour weeks on a frequent basis.

'When I was working for the Philadelphia 76ers, we were in an historic turnaround,' he said. 'We went through a three-year period where we had lost more games [in that timeframe] than any team … in the history of the league. It was bad. We had particularly gotten pounded one night and I came home at 11:30 pm, and my wife heard me stomping around the kitchen. She came down, she's like, "What's going on?" I was like, "What do you mean?" She's like, "You're stomping around here like a child, what's happening?" And I was like, "Did you see our game? Did you hear the boos?" She's said, "I didn't even need the TV on to hear the boos. That's how loud they were." And I said, "Well, I don't understand why you're questioning my mood." She said, "This doesn't work. ... you and your attitude. When you come home here, I need a husband, I need a father. I don't need this. So, you got to find a way."'

It was clear that the expectations and stressors of Scott's career were starting to impact his personal life and relationships. He wasn't doing well at creating boundaries between work and life. And so a friend of his came up with a great solution that had been working well for him. 'A dear friend of mine said, "It's the easiest thing in the world,"' Scott told me. 'I said, "Easiest?" I said, "For me, it's the hardest." He said, "No, I have this tree out back my house and I pull up my driveway, I get out of my car, put my hand on the tree. It's a worry tree, all my worries go through the tree, and I walk in the house, I'm good to go."'

Scott got the point and started to create simple habits to ensure that he was enforcing healthy boundaries between work and life. 'When I turn into the driveway, that's my trigger. Work is over at that point. And I walk in as Dad. One of the tricks of the trade for me is to keep my phone in the car for the first couple of hours once I get home.' He admitted that it's not easy – in fact, it can be difficult at times. How often do you work on your phone or device at home? But setting the boundary *and* enforcing it as Scott did is the key to high performance. Say no to your distractions. Say no to work when you're with your loved ones.

Scott told me that when he was at the helm of Madison Square Garden there were major events every night of the week and he found it hard not to show up to them. But at a certain point, his body started to tell him to slow down. He shared a simple yet powerful tool that many high performers implement: 'Don't be a slave to your text or emails. Please don't pick up your phone first thing in the morning, or check your emails and texts. If you do, you're now on somebody else's schedule and somebody else's agenda. Instead, have an intention for the day, have three things you want to accomplish in a day. And make sure you do those before getting lost in your emails.'

Scott is also committed to enforcing boundaries with meetings. He said he decided at one point to automatically reduce all 60-minute meetings to 30 minutes, and then reduce any 30-minute meetings to 15 minutes. Right away, he had more time. And it forced all meeting participants to be prepared, focused and respectful of time.

Set boundaries and enforce them

Here's my challenge to you: become a boundary boss. Self-discipline is an essential component of a life well lived, and non-negotiable for people who want to unleash their true potential. Supercharging your self-talk (as you did earlier in this chapter) and focusing on your priorities (as you will in the next) will elevate your performance significantly, but if you cannot master boundary enforcement, your efforts will be hindered.

Setting *and* enforcing boundaries is a crucial trait in your pursuit of personal excellence. If mastery is a must in your life, then you will need to say no a lot more. And I mean a *lot* more.

When I started out in my speaking and coaching career, I'd jump at every opportunity. I was the yes wizard, casting spells of agreement on every request that appeared. It certainly led to a jam-packed calendar, but also a lot more stress. I was the boss of busy being busy. I lacked clear priorities and had a very vague vision. The result: a few years of treading water. If I could rewind the clock, I'd go back to those years and breathe. Stop for a minute. Get clear on my priorities in relation to my Altair. And become a boss at saying no.

In recent years, I've stayed more congruent to my long-game goals, which has led to a lot more nos to social occasions that I don't really want to attend, to clients that I don't really love serving and to opportunities that dilute my focus. It has been difficult, almost awkward at times. Saying yes is part of my lifelong disease to please. In a self-assessment of my personality, 'seeking harmony' was one of the traits that sat in the top five. It sounds rather positive, but it means I often want to keep multiple people happy at once, just to avoid upsetting the apple cart.

There's no pain inside our own comfort zone, but growth and joy exist in doing hard things. Saying no to people and opportunities is hard for me, and possibly you too. Identifying where I needed to set and enforce boundaries has given me countless more hours with my loved ones, abundantly more energy and a much more successful business. It has also meant that I don't see some friends quite as much as I did, and that my calendar isn't booked from morning till night. I've let go of identifying my worth by how busy I am and how many friends I catch up with each week. I have a small inner circle of trusted friends. I connect with each of them often, and our conversations are deep and inspiring. I'd much rather that than small talk, gossip and drinking at the pub. But that's just me. Finding your happy balance is your own personal mission.

Steve Jobs was undoubtedly one of the world's high performers. He changed the face of the technology world and his relentless commitment to excellence was matched only by his disciplined approach to the things that mattered most. I once chatted to his executive assistant, Naz Beheshti, who spoke of how strict Jobs was with his calendar. He would be very firm about meeting times, would often host those meetings while walking, and would prioritise yoga, meditation and wholefood meals.

There's often a pattern like this with the global game-changers, where they set very strict guidelines. Every prime minister I've ever worked with has had a gatekeeper, a person who stands firm to ensure that only the people who align with their mission are allowed into the calendar. When I did my first ever interview with a head of state, I couldn't believe it when his secretary said I had 25 minutes. I simply couldn't understand how an effective conversation could happen in such a short time. But it forced me to focus only on the important points and I got way more wisdom than I'd bargained for – because he was in the habit of doing the same.

But what *is* a boundary? Effective personal boundaries balance protection and connection, functioning like a selectively permeable stone wall whose gate allows us control over our emotional and mental space. Boundaries require clear, reasonable limits that respect our personal needs and those of others, focusing on authenticity and reality rather than emotional reactions. The necessary starting point is giving yourself permission to set limits, understanding your personal thresholds, being mindful about sharing information, and clearly communicating your needs. If you want the ultimate relationship enhancement and self-perception boost, set yourself some boundaries. Healthy boundaries are the limits you place around your emotions, time, body and mindset to stay content with who you are. These 'fences' protect you from being used, manipulated or drained by others.

Using emotional leverage to control boundaries

Some people are motivated by a future-positive state, a time to come that looks optimistic and hopeful. But many humans are driven by the avoidance of pain. They will literally do anything to avoid suffering. Let's use this to our advantage by putting some emotional leverage on ourselves. Essentially, we want to have an emotional relationship, or connection, to our desired outcomes.

I had a coaching client in America who was struggling to enforce boundaries at work. She was the yes-woman who would do anything for anyone at the cost of her own time and sanity. I asked her what her life would be like five years from then if she continued to be busy being busy. What she shared sounded like a mental-health jail sentence. Just taking the time to bring her potential future pain into the present allowed her to feel the suffering physically and emotionally. Then I asked her what would cause her acute pain in the short term, to use as a negative consequence if she failed to enforce a boundary.

She concluded that donating money to her least preferred political party would cause her a lot of discomfort. She then made a commitment to donate $50 to this party every time she lacked boundary enforcement, but when we explored a little deeper we discovered that $50 really wasn't that painful. She said she could do that once or twice a week and it wouldn't make a dent in her wallet. So I asked her to multiply it by ten. Now, every time she dropped the ball on her boundaries, she would have to donate $500 to her most despised political party. Guess what? She never broke that boundary ever again. She used self-imposed leverage to multiply her emotional connection to her desired outcome.

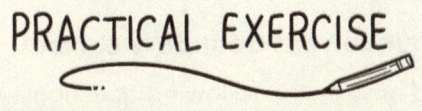

IDENTIFY, SET AND ENFORCE BOUNDARIES

If you're unwilling to improve your boundary enforcement skills, then you're willing to forfeit your dream outcomes. You're not here to give up on your goals, so let's get cracking.

I use the following exercise in the personal mastery and high-performance leadership events I host. It's a simple yet powerful exercise designed to help you identify where you most require boundaries and plan how to enforce them.

But let's stop for a second and ask, 'Why should I bother doing this exercise? Will boundary-setting have any impact on my life or career?' The research suggests that it will.

Lacking clear work–life boundaries increases emotional exhaustion and reduces happiness. In addition, a lack of professional boundaries multiplies stress, heightens susceptibility to burnout and leaves individuals open to increased boundary violations, which will clearly impact their wellbeing. At a family level, in particular in your closest relationships, not being clear with boundaries can lead to privacy invasions, increased turmoil and potential conflict. Optimal psychological boundaries are dynamic, allowing for healthy interactions with others while preserving personal integrity and autonomy. Inadequate boundaries can lead to psychological issues.

Step 1: Think about your current boundary control
Take out your journal and answer the following questions:
- Where do I struggle to say no?
- Who tends to take up a lot of my energy?
- Where do I spend time (or money) that I know I shouldn't?

Step 2: Decide where you need boundaries
Take a moment to get clear on what specific areas of your life require boundaries and pop them in your journal.

Perhaps it's boundaries relating to people you spend time with. Maybe it's boundaries around specific habits you have? Or it could even pertain to boundaries around what you say yes to in your professional life.

Step 3: Find your emotional leverage for boundary control

Remember my client who decided to donate to her most despised political party whenever she lost control of her boundaries? Now it's your turn. First, let's talk about how to actually enforce them. Setting a boundary and enforcing it are two totally different things.

Here are a few key ingredients of effective boundary setting:

1. Tell the other person what *you* are going to do, not what *they* should do.
2. Introduce limits and don't explain why.
3. Make it about *you and your limits* – *not* about them or what's best for them.

To do this you will need to take the following action.

Plan your no ahead of time

If someone asks you for a meeting, invites you to a party or asks for your time, then I would suggest that you consider responding with, 'Would you mind texting or emailing me so I can look at my calendar and come back to you?' or say yes in principle, as I did with the Kolisi Foundation, and that you will confirm with them later. This gives you some time to think about whether you truly want, or need, to commit. Some of us find saying no in the moment, face to face, very challenging. As I mentioned earlier, my desire to seek harmony in social settings has led to a lot of difficulty in saying no over the years. By asking for some time to look at your calendar, you create space for yourself to enforce a boundary if required.

Don't offer an explanation
Okay, this is the tricky part. More often than not, we feel compelled to offer up an explanation as to why we're saying no. Many of us resort to, 'I can't [insert the thing they want from you] because [insert your excuse].' You might be tempted to say, 'I can't come to your party because I can't get a babysitter in time,' but this leaves the conversation open for the other person to argue and challenge your excuse. They might say, 'I've got you covered, my niece is looking for babysitting jobs and she's available.' The solution is to say, 'Thank you, but no, I can't make it.'

Propose an alternative
If you still want to be connected with the person you're saying no to, you might consider offering another time to catch up. 'Sorry, I can't make it to your birthday. Would you like to have dinner the following week?'

Why boundaries are so important
To sum up, people who consistently enforce boundaries tend to have lower levels of stress and elevated self-esteem because

they prioritise their space, time and mental wellbeing. People who lack boundary skills can be manipulated into doing things they really don't want to do, often at the expense of their health, their time and sometimes even their safety. In work or in your personal relationships, poor boundaries can lead to resentment, anger and burnout.

At different stages in life you might find yourself having to set and enforce new boundaries. For example, in my late teens and early twenties, I always gave an emphatic yes to any party invitation. It didn't matter what night of the week it was, I was committed to my social life. Now, though, as a partner, parent and business owner, I'm much more protective of my leisure time. More often than not, I say no to evening functions because I want to spend the time with the people who matter most – my family (and pets!). For years I found it very difficult to say no to people when they invited me to parties, dinners or weddings, but in recent times I've become comfortable with this mantra: 'Thank you so much for inviting me, but I'm unable to make it. I hope the event goes great.' As the years pass by, perhaps my stance will change again, but for now my leisure time is precious and well protected.

Many of us struggle with setting limits and, without a plan, often fall back on the same unproductive methods – either doubling down or caving in. We often have a nagging worry that drawing lines might come off as harsh or self-centred, but the truth is that not setting them is what's truly harmful. If you want to be a high performer, you need to get comfortable with saying no. Boundaries are like safeguards for our connections – they're about ensuring we're taken care of first, rather than being insincere, brewing resentment and eventually feeling trapped. So now that you have the right strategies, it's time to step up and take control.

* * *

Saying no is the secret to success in high performance. The challenge is to discipline your inner domain so you can dominate the outer domain. Stay vigilant with the words you say to yourself and ensure you don't get caught in the trap of getting busy being busy.

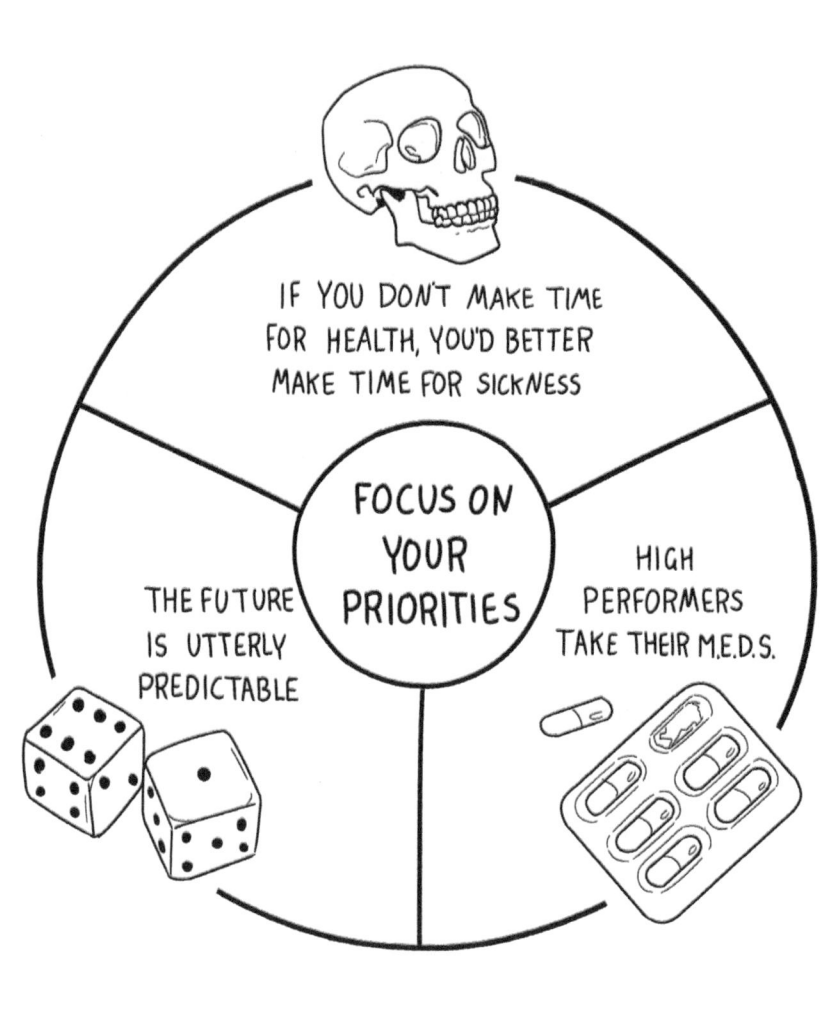

6
FOCUS ON YOUR PRIORITIES

Over the years, countless leaders have approached me for executive coaching. One of the most commonly shared challenges among them was their discontent with their own physical and, at times, mental health. I've often witnessed that the most driven performers on field can be the most passive performers off field. They go the extra mile with their work, but find every excuse with their personal wellbeing.

Ryan was the best performer in his entire industry nationwide. He brought home millions and did so over many consecutive years. He was regarded as a high performer by all of his peers and competitors, except for one area: his health. I made it abundantly clear that if he wanted better results in all aspects of his life, then he needed to make some changes. It took some time, but he began to realise that if he didn't make time for health, he'd have to make time for sickness.

When I first asked him to start prioritising his health, I was met with resistance. Ryan felt that time spent on exercise was time lost on writing more business. He understood numbers, so I needed to speak to him in his language. I presented him with a thought often attributed to Albert Einstein: 'Compound interest is the eighth wonder of the world. He who understands it, earns it; he who doesn't, pays it.' Of course it pertains to money, but it equally applies to our health. If we make small deposits each day through movement, nutrition and rest, we will start to pave the path to a longer and healthier life.

Once Ryan embraced the fact that he needed to focus on his priorities, he was all in. But he was so eager that he wanted to make multiple changes and establish several habits all at once. As you might have experienced yourself, this sort of shortcut rarely works. I've had several Januarys where I bought a gym membership, started waking at 4.30 am, juiced twice a day and stopped eating chocolate. Fast forward two or three weeks and I'd pretty much quit on all of it. Can you think of a time when you've tried to make positive changes to your life but struggled to maintain them? Well, you're not alone.

Time and time again, more than 70 per cent of adults start their year with a resolution and 55 per cent of them believe they will stick to it. Often, a large percentage can maintain the new habit or habits for a week or three. But research shows that two years later, less than 20 per cent have made them stick.

I had Ryan slow things down and get clear on where he most needed to direct his attention in terms of priorities and habits. Then we set out to change one thing at a time with a specific method for establishing habits. We're going to do exactly the same thing for you over the next few pages.

Here's why you should spend valuable time fine-tuning your habits. A study of more than 330,000 European adults found that a lack of physical activity may lead to twice as many deaths as those from obesity. It also found that a slight increase in physical activity could have huge health benefits. The study leader, Professor Ulf Ekelund, shared a powerful insight: 'Just a small amount of physical activity each day could have substantial health benefits for people who are physically inactive. Although we found that just 20 minutes would make a difference, we should really be looking to do more than this – physical activity has many proven health benefits and should be an important part of our daily life.'

Some of our focus must be on physical health, but we must also prioritise rest, nutrition, connection and other important factors. The point I want you to embrace in this chapter is that high performers are incredibly consistent in focusing on their priorities.

In this chapter, we're going to explore three principles:

23. If you don't make time for health, you'd better make time for sickness.

24. High performers take their MEDS (mental training, exercise, diet and sleep).
25. The future is utterly predictable.

Principle 23: If you don't make time for health, you'd better make time for sickness

Well-maintained habits promote a life of longevity. The opposite guarantees a life of brevity. We are creatures of habit. Some say that by the time we are 35 years old, a vast part of who we are is a memorised set of behaviours, emotional reactions, unconscious habits, hardwired attitudes, beliefs and perceptions that function like a computer program. Most of our reactions are therefore automated habits, leaving us with just a small percent of our conscious mind to think outside the mould we've created for ourselves. Our micro-habits dictate our macro lives. In fact, our days are our life in miniature. The things we eat, drink, watch and do are shaping us in every moment of every day. The people we choose to cohabit or work with will shape our daily habits more powerfully than we can begin to imagine. If you're committed to taking things to the next level, then to help you make it a reality you will need to commit to refining your habits.

I caught up with a friend for lunch several years back. His life was somewhat different to mine – our ambitions were radically different. While mine was to help great humans become the greatest in their chosen field of endeavour, his was to become the greatest athlete of all time in his sport.

We sat down to lunch shortly after he'd done several hours of intense training with his teammates. I ordered falafel salad with peppermint tea and he ordered a cheeseburger, fries and a glass of cola. As he consumed it, all I could think about was his lack of commitment to good eating habits. When I gently asked about his meal, he made it abundantly clear that for him it was about trying to get as many calories in as possible, as his body simply needed to replenish what it had used up.

If I ate that sort of meal regularly I'd be out of shape and feeling the worse for wear. But that wasn't the case for him. The important point here is that habits are personal and should be selected based on your desired outcome: your El Capitan. Scrolling through social media and seeing a post that reads 'Oprah Winfrey's Top 5 Habits' should be a signal to you to keep scrolling. Oprah's habits serve *her* mission, not yours. We should each take some time to craft compelling habits that will move *us* towards the next level.

What is a habit?

Before we go on, it's crucial that we agree on some of the critical components that make up a habit. In its simplest form, a habit is something someone does often in a regular and repeated way, almost without thinking. This makes it something that's hard to stop doing. You and I are continuously and repeatedly performing one habit after another – our wake-up time, our morning coffee, our teeth-brushing commitment, driving our cars, our daily food habits and so on. Some of our habits are good for us, others not so much.

A habit is either empowering or disempowering. We want the former – habits that help us grow in a healthy way towards a meaningful outcome. Habits like exercise, a balanced diet, social connection and meaningful work are all empowering. But we can also overexercise, count calories, avoid solitude and become obsessed with working. It's easy for an empowering habit to become a disempowering one relatively quickly. In this chapter, I'm going to share a tool that will help you to maintain some sense of balance when it comes to developing good habits.

The habit loop

Before we dive into habit formation, let's first take a look at the neuroscience behind it all. I had a conversation recently with a self-made multibillionaire, a fascinating character. One of the most compelling views he shared with me was that he takes time to research each aspect of the business deeply before hiring somebody else to do it. Rather than outsource from the outset, he takes the time to gain a broad understanding of the situation and sets out to build his own view and solution. It seems to have served him well – so much so that he handled his first initial public offering when he floated his company, without any specialist advisers or brokers. This is arguably an unheard of and highly unorthodox approach, but it worked well for him, and the company value has skyrocketed over months and years.

I'm going to ask you to take a leaf from this man's book, and gain a deeper understanding of habits before we get to the fun part of establishing your very own high-performance habits.

At the core of habit formation is a three-part loop consisting of:

1. a cue – a trigger for the behaviour
2. a behaviour – the routine itself
3. a reward – a positive reinforcement for the behaviour.

If you want to ensure a habit sticks, it's important to create a conducive environment for the new habit, engage in regular routine repetition and achieve a sense of harmony or satisfaction from the activity.

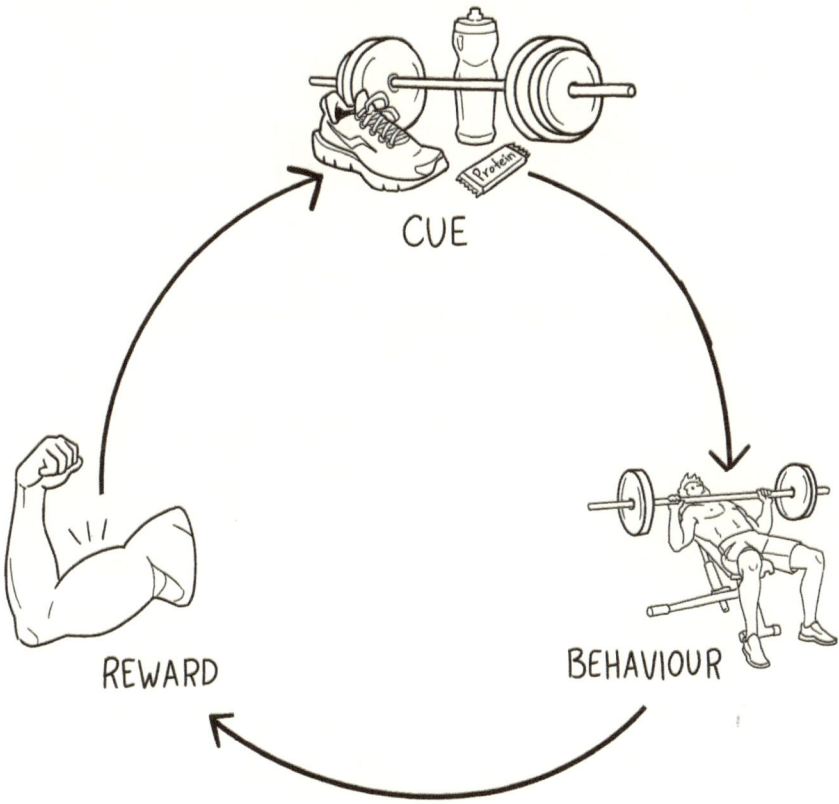

The cue

First, let's look at the starting point of habit formation, the trigger or 'cue'. This is the point at which the new habit begins to fire. Bestselling author of *Atomic Habits* James Clear defines five core types of cue:

1. time
2. location
3. preceding events
4. emotional state
5. other people.

Each trigger offers a unique approach to cueing new habits, whether it's a specific time of day, the environment you're in, an event that just happened, how you feel, or the influence of those around you. Clear emphasises the importance of choosing a specific and actionable cue for your new habit in order to ensure it's successful.

Let's look at each cue in detail, so that you can see how it works in your existing – and future – habits.

1. Time

Habits can be triggered at certain times of day. For example, drinking a glass of water right after waking up, taking a walk every day at lunchtime or reading before bed. Other examples might be setting a reminder to stretch every hour during work, having tea at 4 pm or writing a to-do list before bed.

How I use it: Every morning, as soon as I wake up, often between 5.30 and 6.00, I reach for my journal before I step out of bed. I use this time to practise gratitude and clarify my MVP for the day.

2. Location

Our environment can cue certain habits. This might be using the act of entering the gym as a cue to start a workout, opening a book every time you sit on your porch, tidying up when entering the kitchen or organising your desk as a cue to start work.

How I use it: Each time I get into my car and close the door, it's my cue to lift my phone and choose a podcast or audio book to listen to (unless my son is in the car – then we pump up the music!). I do this so that I can continue to grow and learn.

3. Preceding events

One action can trigger the next habit. This might be, for example, brushing your teeth after finishing breakfast, stretching after turning off your computer or meditating after journaling.

How I use it: A super simple one for me is, after I brush my teeth and get into bed in the evening, I lift the book off my bedside table and read a few pages. This usually leads to me reading several more pages or a whole chapter. This automatically ensures that I add a little bit of learning, escaping or relaxing right before I nod off.

4. Emotional state

Feelings can prompt habits, such as going for a run when stressed, calling a friend when you're feeling lonely or practising deep breathing when anxious.

How I use it: As I'm approaching a stadium or convention centre to deliver a speech, I use the natural nervousness I feel in my throat to trigger some slow and deliberate breathwork exercises. It brings my heart rate down and allows me to walk on stage feeling comfortable and calm.

5. Other people

Those around us can influence our habits. An example might include joining a colleague for a healthy lunch, biking with a friend on weekends or attending a study group.

How I use it: When I'm meeting friends, I will opt for a walk-and-talk rather than a lunch. If lunch is a necessity, then I will generally (not always!) choose a clean and healthy meal.

The behaviour

This is simply the habit itself, as in your desired activity or action. It may be your 5-kilometre run, writing a paragraph of your upcoming speech, drinking that glass of water once you wake up – or any number of other things you do on the daily. You will likely find it easy to identify the behaviour. The difficult part is sustaining it consistently for long enough for it to become a habit, particularly when friction kicks in. Friction is something uncomfortable that stops the action becoming a habit. It might be something like your phone distracting you, wet weather deterring you from running, or opting for a creamy coffee first thing instead of water.

The reward

We are creatures of habit, but for a habit to stick we must experience a reward. When we genuinely experience a reward, our body releases a shot of dopamine. Dopamine signals a reward and also guides us (and other animals) to home in, through trial and error, on the behaviours that lead to those rewards. In fact, our brain's reward system can directly alter the full range of our movements and behaviours. Why do people keep going back to a gruelling spin class? Because their body gets such a rush of dopamine from the activity. But it's the same reason people go back to sugary foods and develop substance addictions.

When we're trying to establish high-performance habits, it's critical to ensure a dopamine reward as an outcome of performing the action. If we don't reap any benefits or rewards from the behaviour, the chance of it becoming a habit is greatly reduced.

IDENTIFY THREE HABITS YOU WANT TO ESTABLISH

What habits do you need to develop to become the high performer you want to be? It's important that you get specific about your desired outcomes, both personally and professionally. Not everyone has to perform the same way – in fact, the opposite is true.

Take out your journal and think about the actions or behaviours you need to cultivate in order to move towards your El Cap. Often they will be simple and commonsense behaviours or actions. For example, if you want to achieve a monumental career goal, perhaps you need to be more effective with your time. So a new habit would be to spend time at the end of each day planning out the following day and scheduling actions on your calendar. After all, what gets scheduled gets done.

Starting with the end in mind is always an approach that high performers adopt, so I urge you to think about what you're trying to achieve and then identify what daily or weekly behaviours will move you towards that goal. It may be exercise, nutrition, learning, thinking, speaking or any other number of things that will drive the outcome you want.

If you need to get a whole lot of ideas down and take time to work through them to come up with your three habits, then do that. There's no point trying to establish a habit you don't need, so if it takes you a week to identify your desired habits, then so be it.

Why only three habits? Well, research has shown that we can manage to develop no more than three new habits at once. Try any more than three and you will fail at all of them. I actually recommend only trying one at a time. This is why you want to make sure you identify the best habits you need to develop right now in order to move towards your El Cap.

If you're having trouble working out what your habits should be, don't worry. The next exercise will help you with that.

Principle 24: High performers take their MEDS

George Russell is a high-performance athlete, racing on Formula One circuits year after year. Like his competitors, he's always looking for that high-performance edge. In this way, he is no different from you and me. We're all looking for that competitive edge, whether it be in our career, chosen sport or health.

I invited George's coach, Aleix Casanovas, onto my podcast to look deeper at the things George prioritises. Aleix is one of the world's leading performance coaches and is always on the lookout for tools and habits that will help give his clients a winning advantage. When we got specific about George's mental and physical habits, Aleix made it clear that meditation and sleep were just as important as nutrition and exercise.

'I plan naps throughout the day. And meditation is such a powerful tool. Naps will have a positive impact on performance, and meditation will improve decision-making. If George isn't sleepy he will meditate, and if he's sleepy he'll take a nap.'

Aleix acknowledged that the cultural norms where he grew up, in Spain, accepted and embraced siestas. And that because it's not part of English culture, it was more challenging to convince George on the nap front. 'There's that view that you're lazy if you take a nap,' Aleix said. 'Actually, it's completely the opposite. We perform much better and we know his reaction time improves.'

We can all influence the quality of our sleep, and George takes this to the next level. Aleix shared that they fly his mattress, pillow and duvet to every race to ensure he has the best possible sleep environment. It's clear to me that George takes his MEDS seriously.

What are MEDS? They are:

- Mental training
- Exercise
- Diet
- Sleep

This kind of dedication to optimising all aspects of an athlete's routine is something that can be adapted to various high-performance settings. And it can most certainly be adopted by everyday people too.

You and I might not be flying around a racecourse at breakneck speed, but we still need to perform at our best. If we want to achieve high performance in our work and/or life, then we need to control the controllables. Those controllables are our mental resilience, our physical strength, our nutrition and our sleep quality.

PRACTICAL EXERCISE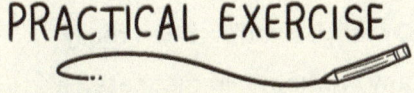

MEDS ASSESSMENT

If you struggled in the previous exercise to identify what high-performance habits you need to adopt, then I'd suggest you do a MEDS assessment. This will help you gain clarity on what might be the best focus for you right now to elevate your performance in life, work or sport. Having worked with and interviewed professional athletes, international leaders, neuroscientists and global experts, I've discovered that thriving high performers generally embrace a number of specific habits, all of which fall into the MEDS categories.

Step 1: Mark your MEDS out of ten

Take out your journal. Think about the past two months, and give yourself a score ranging from 0 to 10 for each MEDS category – 0 for highly unsatisfactory and 10 if you have no room for improvement. Here's how you might go about that:

- **Mental training**: If you regularly take time for breathing exercises (see the downloadable resources), meditation or walking in nature while focusing on your breath, then perhaps you'd score a 9. But if you don't spend any time reflecting, thinking, journaling or meditating, then perhaps you'd score 2 or 3.
- **Exercise**: Maybe you set out to move your body four times a week. If you achieved that more or less consistently over the past two months, then perhaps

you're an 8 out of 10. Or maybe you've been really busy and done hardly any workouts. In that case, you're probably a 2 out of 10.

- **Diet**: Perhaps you decided that you'd have coffee takeaways only on a Saturday, eat plant-based meals two days a week and consume seven glasses of water daily. But maybe you had a few cheeky coffees and shortchanged yourself on the water intake, so you might score 6 out of 10 this month. Or maybe you stuck to your plan and feel great about it, in which case you're a 9 out of 10.
- **Sleep:** Maybe your goal was to maintain a regular bedtime and a regular waking-up time. But you've had a ton of deadlines this last few months and a number of social gatherings so you haven't managed to achieve regular sleeping habits. Give yourself a 2 out of 10. Alternatively, if your goal was to get seven hours' or more sleep per night and you've hit that consistently, you might be a 9.

Step 2: Identify a way to improve

The aim here is to focus on your lowest-scoring area and decide on a simple action to improve it slightly over the next two months. If you try to improve in every area simultaneously, you'll possibly be overwhelmed and more reluctant to take positive action. Complexity kills execution. Keep it simple, and focus on improving your lowest-ranking area.

Focus on Your Priorities

Say my E score was the lowest. I would then focus on some minor, and consistent, changes to my exercise routine over the next eight weeks. Slow change is sustainable, so identify your lowest-ranking area and commit to improvement by picking just one new action or habit. Here are a few examples of what you might do in each area to improve slightly. Don't try to do all of them at once. Pick one and see how the first four weeks go:

- **Mental training**: A two-minute meditation to start off the morning. Box breathing at lunchtime. Lighting a candle and focusing on the flame for one full minute.
- **Exercise**: A morning run. An evening yoga session to unwind. Taking 10,000 steps a day. Four sessions at the gym each week. Five squats after each visit to the toilet.
- **Diet**: Intermittent fasting daily. Two days a week of plant-based meals. Seven glasses of water a day. Three alcohol-free days a week.
- **Sleep**: Consistently go to bed at 9.30 pm. Wear an eye mask. No screens one hour before bed. Breathwork exercises before bed, with extended exhales. No caffeine after 10 am.

Write down your decision in your journal and make sure you implement your new behaviour regularly so that it becomes a habit. Review your progress at one and two months, perhaps even three, until you're sure it's a habit and you're happy with your score out of 10. You can then move on to improve in other areas.

Developing a new habit

Now that you've decided on a habit you want to establish, it's important to get honest with yourself about how long it might take to really embed it. How long do you think it takes to form a new habit? Is it 7 days, 21 days, 28 days or longer? Over the years I've been led to believe that the magic number is 21 days. Why then, did I continuously struggle to develop long-term habits? University College London (UCL) answered that question by conducting a study into habits and debunking my old beliefs. In fact, this study brought to my attention an important word – *automaticity* – that changed the game for me. Automaticity is the point at which you're able to say, 'I do this without having to consciously remember to do it.' Think tying your shoelaces, opening a door or saying hello. You can do these things without consciously reminding yourself how to perform the actions.

UCL found that the point of automaticity was, on average, reached at the 66-day mark. Obviously there were varying outcomes, but the average time taken was just over two months. When it came to establishing new habits, I was often giving up around the one-month mark – which isn't even halfway according to this study.

Why do certain behaviours become habitual? Our brains create habits to conserve energy. The less we have to think about something, the less energy our brain needs to utilise. The brain can save that energy for other functions. When we perform a new habit, we start to create new neurons and neural connections. As we repeatedly perform the activity, these connections are coated in a fatty tissue called myelin. The more myelinated the connection, the less energy required by the brain to perform that action. Your brain will literally prioritise these actions. When I think back to learning to drum, I practised the same movements thousands and thousands of times, to the point where I could perform them competently under pressure while thinking about what I might have for dinner. I wasn't born with some secret sauce or high-performance DNA, I just repeated the action until I reached the point of autopilot (or as we now know, automaticity). Simply put, when tasks become habitual and the brain pathway becomes optimised, the brain uses less energy to perform those tasks thanks to the more efficient transmission of signals.

Here's an extreme example of the power of habit formation. The chief of police in West Auckland, New Zealand, knocked on the door of a local house. He spoke to a single mum about her son who had recently borrowed a motorbike without permission. The boy, who was only 14, attempted to evade the police by ditching the bike and running for his life. He was too fast for the police officers, but not for the German shepherd police dog that tore into his arm and allowed his eventual arrest.

The chief of police was also a track and field coach, so he asked Zion Armstrong's mother if he could mentor him. He hadn't seen anyone run that quickly in quite some time. This intervention at such a pivotal stage in the young boy's life led to him setting a vision for himself to become a champion athlete. He also benefited from an incredible male role model.

This incident set in motion a deliberate commitment to a simple set of habits and routines that helped Zion move closer to his Altair. His disciplined approach to athletics involved intense training and perseverance, often stretching his personal limits. Luck had nothing to do with his progress, yet it might be said that the harder he worked, the luckier he got. He won national titles in the 110- and 400-metre hurdles, breaking the national record in the latter. He represented New Zealand at the World Junior Championships in Lisbon, Portugal, where his relay team finished fourth in the 4 x 400 metres. To top it off, Zion represented New Zealand at the Commonwealth Games in Kuala Lumpur.

How you do anything is how you do everything. What happens in your personal life often translates to what happens in your professional life. Zion, the once troubled young boy from West Auckland, put his mind to an inspiring vision and developed high-performance habits that helped him march slowly towards his El Capitan. If you take a moment to look at how his professional life unfolded, you'll be equally impressed. In fact, Zion worked his way to the top of a household apparel brand, becoming the president of Adidas North America.

Zion's story is a reminder that small things done consistently over the long term lead to incredible results. You are a creature of habit and your days are your life in miniature. The micro-actions you perform each and every day are moving you towards or away from the life you most want. Developing a habit is a choice and only you can choose to do the work. Zion became consistent at focusing on his priorities and understood the power of managing intentional habits.

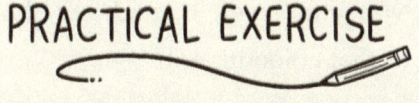 

PRACTICAL EXERCISE

FORM A HABIT THE SIMPLE WAY

Habit installation is a very predictable process. I use this extremely simple approach to help my clients cultivate high-performance habits that stick. Take out your journal and do the following.

Step 1: Analyse the habit you want to form
Write down what your new habit is, then go into detail about the mechanics of it. Remember, vague thinking produces vague results. If it's running, describe the motion, the distance, the timing. If it's a specific skill at work or in the sporting arena, then get granular with the detail. Your subconscious mind thrives on hyper-specificity.

Step 2: Get clear on your why
It's important to define why this new action is important. If you don't have the emotional juice to perform the task, particularly on days when your motivation is waning, then you will simply procrastinate. This is what separates the good from the great. The *greats* do the thing, even when they don't feel like doing it. The *goods* simply give themselves the day off when they're not quite feeling up to it.

Write out a list of reasons why this new action is important to you, your team, your family, your wealth, your joy and anything else that comes to mind. When I decided to try one year of alcohol-free living, I needed an extensive list of reasons why this was important. It made all the difference in me sticking to that commitment.

Step 3: Evaluate the costs of not forming the habit
Leverage is a powerful tool when used to help us achieve empowering outcomes. I want you to get clear now on what it will cost you if you don't embrace the new habit. With the no-alcohol habit I mentioned in Step 2, I identified that not forming the habit would cost me financially, and impact my relationships, my health and even potentially my life. The costs were significant enough for me to really double down on my commitment to the new action.

Step 4: Zero in on a powerful habit trigger
The habit trigger is where most of us trip up. A powerful trigger is essential to us performing the action, so how do we ensure that our trigger is powerful enough? That's easy! We can simply use an existing behaviour to trigger our desired behaviour. What are some things that you, I and most humans on the planet do every day? Wake up, brush our teeth, eat, commute, go to the toilet, sit down, arrive home after a day of work – the list goes on. All of these simple tasks are automated and can act as powerful triggers for your new behaviour. Simply link them.

Focus on Your Priorities

For example, I used to reach for a glass of wine as I cooked dinner. My new approach was to use chopping vegetables as my trigger to pop the kettle on for a cup of tea. I mindfully connected food preparation with turning the kettle on. Remember, complexity kills execution. Keep it simple and try it today – just don't try too many new behaviours at once. Simple existing behaviours are powerful triggers for your new high-performance habits.

Step 5: Identify your reward
Don't forget the fun part – your reward. If we don't have a release of dopamine after the new activity then we're unlikely to activate the habit loop and so we'll multiply our chances of quitting. I've quit new habits many times. If you need to create the reward manually, do it. Perhaps after you perform the action you allow yourself to indulge in a reward, be it watching TV, eating something you love, or making time to relax. If you've gone all the way to habit formation and automaticity, you might give yourself a bigger reward – a new item of clothing, a cheat day or a holiday.

Take your time, but whatever you do please make sure you take your MEDS. If you want to play in the arena of high performance, you'll need the physical and mental fortitude to do so. Because if you don't make time for health, you'll need to make time for sickness.

Principle 25: The future is utterly predictable

You can predict your future. As a species, we're set up to create how our future reality unfolds. I'm not talking about manifestation. I'm talking about the fact that we have hardware that gives us an advantage. Our brain is set up for us to shape future outcomes.

When we repeat a behaviour, our brain simultaneously strengthens the neural connections involved through a process called synaptic strengthening, and prunes away unused connections through synaptic pruning. This makes habitual behaviours more automatic over time. We might want to develop new habits by strengthening neural connections, but sometimes we want to focus on eliminating an unhealthy habit instead.

Dr Gina Cleo, author of *The Habit Revolution*, has a PhD in habits. On my podcast, she shared with me that when we want to break an unwanted habit, the goal is to reduce the frequency of the behaviour. This in turn weakens the associated neural pathways, which over a period of time are pruned away, making the habit significantly less automatic.

Dr Cleo highlighted that one of the most effective ways to break an unwanted habit is to eliminate the trigger that prompts the behaviour. So if the bottle of wine sitting in your fridge door is the trigger, simply ensure you don't have any alcohol in your house. That level of friction will help you break your unwanted habit of overconsuming alcohol.

Take a moment to think about a habit you'd like to eliminate. Perhaps it's an eating habit in the evenings, or an addiction to your phone. Then work backwards to identify what the trigger is that makes you perform that behaviour. Two strong triggers that get you to pick up your phone, for example, are the ding of a notification or simply boredom. So perhaps turning off notifications and creating a list of other things to do to stave off your boredom would be a good start in eliminating those triggers.

Replacing old habits with new ones

To replace old habits with new empowering ones, it's important to consistently practise the new behaviour in response to the old trigger. This will strengthen new neural pathways while allowing the old ones to be pruned away and weakened. While your El Capitan is ambitious by design, the key here is to start small. Very small. Infinitesimally small is preferable. When you start with small, bite-sized chunks, it's so much more manageable and reduces friction. If you decide to start with a 10-kilometre run after a decade of no running, you're likely setting yourself up for failure. The same as aiming for million-dollar revenue months when the most you've had so far are $10,000 months. Embrace small steps, daily. Habit installation is about being habitual, not heroic, and common sense isn't always common practice.

One of the hardest habits for me to break was enjoying a beer or wine several times a week. Socialising, entertaining, relaxing, celebrating and connecting were all triggers for me to imbibe. So I took the advice of the neuroscientists and habit experts by ensuring that I had substitutes for my usual tipple.

Suddenly I was a connoisseur of zero per cent beers, wines and gins. And I began to develop a liking for tea, copious amounts of the stuff in fact. I started small by focusing on each day rather than an entire year of alcohol-free living. I could manage one day, then another and another. And eventually this tiny daily action became a newly ingrained habit.

Turning a high-performance technique into a habit
When working with athletes and other high performers, I often equip them with grounding and anchoring techniques that will enhance their performance. I do this by turning these techniques into habits. These same techniques help equally well in the sports arena and the boardroom.

Take my professional rugby player clients, for example. Many players struggle to regulate their emotional arousal throughout the full 80 minutes of a game. If their energy spikes too high, they risk making impulsive mistakes; if it drops too low, their performance suffers. To counter this, we develop a neurolinguistic anchoring technique – a mental and physical cue – that allows them to control their emotional state in real time.

Here's how it works: we identify a specific state the player wants to access – whether it's calm focus, aggression or heightened confidence. Then we link this state to a physical action, such as pressing their big toe into the ground or clenching their fist. The key is to perform this physical action while fully immersed in the desired state, often using visualisation and self-talk. For example, a player might recall their best-ever performance, feeling every detail – the crowd, the adrenaline, the precise execution of their skills – while pressing their toe into the ground. They might also pair it with a phrase like 'I am composed under pressure,' or 'I dominate every play.'

The first few times, the brain doesn't respond, and nothing happens. By the tenth repetition, there's still little noticeable change. But after weeks of daily reinforcement, this small action becomes a powerful habit – one that allows them to shift their emotional state on demand.

I used this exact technique when I performed on stage to win my first world title, and I still use it today when speaking to large audiences. When I need to transition into a high-performance state, I press my toe into the ground and recall a moment of peak performance. My brain has been conditioned to respond instantly.

How you can apply this technique

Develop your own anchoring technique by following these steps:

1. **Choose your desired state:** What emotional state do you want to access on demand? It could be confidence, calmness, focus or even aggression.
2. **Select a physical anchor:** Pick a subtle movement such as pressing your fingers together, clenching your fist or pressing your toe into the ground.

3. **Recall a peak moment:** Close your eyes and vividly relive a time when you felt that state completely. Feel the emotions, hear the sounds and immerse yourself in the moment.
4. **Link the action to the state:** While fully in that emotional state, perform your chosen physical action. Repeat it multiple times, reinforcing the connection.
5. **Repeat:** Practice this daily, ideally when you're in the desired state naturally. Over time, your brain will associate the physical anchor with the emotional response.

Like any habit, this takes time. But once conditioned, it becomes a powerful tool – one you can use before big meetings, presentations, competitions, or any high-stakes moments. Mastery doesn't come from knowing; it comes from doing, again and again.

Neurons that fire together, wire together

Neuroscience shows that when two neurons are activated together frequently, the connection between them becomes stronger. This is the foundation of forming new habits. In simple terms, it's the consistent repetition of a behaviour in response to a specific trigger.

It's time now for you to choose which habits you want to establish and which habits you want to break. You now have the tools and the neuroscience-backed insights you need to move forward. My advice would be to keep it simple and stick to one habit at a time. Spend a few months developing or breaking a habit rather than trying to integrate several new habits all at once. Ensure that you start with the end in mind, working backwards from your desired outcomes in work and life, to define the essential habits you need in order to march steadily towards your goal.

If you're serious about high performance, then embrace Norwegian explorer Roald Amundsen's 20-mile march approach. In the early 1900s, Amundsen, having already been the first to reach the North Pole, was racing to be the first to the South Pole. He was trying to beat Englishman Captain Robert Scott, whose approach was to factor in the weather and adjust accordingly. Amundsen, however, stayed true to his approach of marching 20 miles a day, whatever the conditions. This habit made all the difference, ensuring that he and his team reached the South Pole first. Sadly, Captain Scott and his team all perished on the ice.

The lesson here is that staying committed to a disciplined and steady approach is often a recipe for success. If you still need convincing, just remember Aesop's fable of the hare and the tortoise. Mammoth goals require a steady pace. The bigger the dream, the slower the speed.

Decide on your habits. Schedule them. Do the work. Repeat.

7

TAKE NO SHORTCUTS

Over the years, I've had the privilege of coaching and training thousands of aspiring high performers. After high-performance events I can sense the energy and motivation from the vast majority of attendees, but I know that a huge percentage will not take sustained action towards their dream outcomes. Why? Well, they return to busy being busy. The world is designed to ensure we are back on the hamster wheel chasing our tails.

The small number who take the high-performance principles on board and integrate them into their lives are the ones who are committed to doing the work. They have a plan and they reverse-engineer it to ensure they know their most important next step. The people who focus on the 33rd step are the ones who get stuck in the cycle of procrastination. Complexity kills execution. If you're serious about high performance, please take the time now to break your outcomes down into manageable chunks, so that you can keep taking micro-steps towards success.

Pete is the perfect example. The CEO of a university programme for entrepreneurs, he attended one of my high-performance leadership events that doubles down on personal growth. At the culmination of the event, he could run no more than 5 kilometres. But he committed to reverse-engineering his big goals down into micro-goals. Within a matter of months he had completed his first ultramarathon. A typical week for Pete now involves 80 kilometres of running, including at least two half-marathons. The audacious is within your reach only if you're willing to take no shortcuts. Satisfaction is attained through commitment to doing hard things.

What are you going to do now that you've almost finished this book? Read to the end then pop it back on the shelf? Or commit to making your high-performance life a reality? We look up to role models like Mandela, Phelps, Oprah and Branson. What we admire most is not their ambition, but their commitment to self-mastery. We respect their self-awareness and their ability to do the work even when they don't feel like doing it.

The people I most love and admire as mentors or exemplars are those who did it tough. Those who struggled. Those who developed patience. Those who stayed the course. Those who remained true to their values. At times those get-famous-quick influencers seem strangely appealing. We look at them and think for a moment how great it would be to be like them. The same goes for those drug-addicted rock stars who seem to get what they want when they want. Or those people who make billions on dodgy crypto schemes. It seems easier to be them, almost fulfilling or fun in some way.

But don't be fooled. The person who takes the shortcut pays the price. Nobody feels less fulfilled than the lazy. Nobody feels more self-loathing than the glutton. Nobody feels more fraudulent than the imposter. No matter what praise they might receive from the outside for their outward successes, on the inside they feel empty.

Taking no shortcuts means taking the stairs. It means delaying gratification. It means making a plan to perform specific actions, then actually following through and performing them.

In this chapter, we revise what we've learnt so far in order to look more deeply into our last hurdle – this approach of taking no shortcuts. In doing so, we're going to uncover the essential tenets for bringing high performance to life. For this to become a reality for you, you must embrace the following two principles:

26. Success can be reversed-engineered.
27. The best place to start is at the beginning.

Principle 26: Success can be reverse-engineered

Starting with the end in mind is common sense yet rarely common practice. We find ourselves busy being busy, chasing our tails and saying yes to all the shiny objects. High performers know how critical it is to define their end goal deeply then methodically work backwards from there. Reverse-engineering your desired outcome – rather than haphazardly deciding from moment to moment what your next move might be – ensures that your daily actions are focused on forward movement.

Let's talk about Scott O'Neil once again. Imagine you're the president of Madison Square Garden, or the CEO of the 76ers NBA team, or maybe even heading up the New York Knicks basketball team. You'd be at the helm of some significant organisations with a ton of responsibility and a thousand possible things to focus on at any one time. Scott assumed all these roles and the responsibilities that came with them. We once had a conversation about his approach to making it all work, both on and off the court.

Scott used reverse-engineering on many occasions during his career, and his resume boasts a plethora of household brands. He would look at the CEO role he desired, outline the skills, experiences and network he needed to get that role, then make deliberate steps towards acquiring them. A moment arrived when he decided he was going to use exactly the same process with his family life. He decided on what great looked like, then got clear on what needed to happen to make it a reality. He consulted friends, mentors and coaches to help him stay on track, and moved towards a better balance across the key pillars of his life. His approach was methodical, and he always kept the end in mind. In his bestselling book

Be Where Your Feet Are, Scott wrote, 'Do it right, and you will find yourself digging deep inside. How you live is truly a choice. What you're going to do and who you are going to do it with, those are choices only you can make.' Being intentional about your goals and the discipline you need to achieve them is fully within your control. But they will require your absolute focus and commitment to make them a reality.

Start from your goal and work backwards

When people talk to me about planning their future dreams and goals, they often make the excuse 'I'm too busy.' They make the same excuse when it comes to self-evaluation and prioritising action lists – they claim they simply don't have the time. But if you're too busy to plan, you'd better get busy preparing for mediocre outcomes. When you dilute your focus, you dilute your results.

High performers begin with a clear and purposeful goal, defining what they aspire to become or accomplish. Then they map out a plan to get themselves there, working backwards from the outcome to the first step they need to take. A plan will require you to perform specific actions and behaviours that align with your dream outcome. It boils down to two simple actions: get radically clear and reverse-engineer. No rocket science. No thesis. Just the essentials. High performers simplify their way to success.

The legendary Sir Steve Hansen, former head coach of the All Blacks, once told me how he set the bar for when he took over from Sir Graham Henry, right after they had won the 2011 World Cup. Arguably, there's no greater accomplishment in global rugby than lifting the Webb Ellis Cup. Where does a team go from there? Steve decided he needed to set the team a new El Capitan. Great leaders know that celebrating your victory for too long leads to complacency and eventual decline. In Steve's words, 'We'd just won the World Cup when I took over the team. I knew I'd be asked where I planned to take the team. My response was simple, "Let's be the most dominant team in the history of the game." The coaches liked it, as did the players. We didn't know if it was possible, but we knew it wouldn't be if we didn't try.'

The new vision Steve set was simple in words yet monumental in nature. He threw down the gauntlet for each and every member of the team to join him in trying to rewrite the history books. Aspirational in its very essence, this new goal created a powerful wave of momentum and commitment across the players and management.

As the next eight years unfolded, the results started to reflect the challenge Hansen had set. Under his leadership, in 2016 the team became the first in the professional era to complete a season unbeaten. His record was staggering, in fact: eight Bledisloe Cup wins, six Rugby Championships (against the highest-ranked southern hemisphere teams) and of course the all-important 2015 World Cup. He also amassed four World Rugby Coach of the Year awards. If ever there was an example that vision precedes victory, this might just be it. Steve got clear on the destination, then worked back step by step to outline the plan and strategy to bring it to fruition. He reverse-engineered a record-breaking outcome, with a radically clear vision and a detailed roadmap.

Without a vision, people lack the motivation to go the extra mile. It's crucially important that you have a clear vision of where you are heading in your life, work and relationships. If you're vague, expect vague results.

Be a one-percenter

Most people have good intentions, but good intentions that aren't followed by good actions are simply grand gestures. Why do so many well-meaning humans not do the things they know they should be doing? (I was the same for many years with exercise and alcohol.) The simple answer is they feel overwhelmed. Too many options can make us complacent. The key advantage that high performers have is the ability to focus on their end outcome and work back to their most important next step.

Bestselling author Jay Papasan, shared with me on my podcast that he calls it 'goal-setting to the now'. The overarching question that sums up his great book, co-authored with Gary Keller, *The ONE Thing*, is 'What's the ONE thing I can do now that will make everything else easier or unnecessary?' Jay suggested we might ask ourselves, 'Based on where I want to be in five years, what would I have to accomplish this year?' But he advises, 'Instead of saying "based on where I want to be in five years", you want to keep pulling it closer. You need to say "based on whatever I do in one year, what do I have to do this month; based on what I want to do this month, what I do I need to do this week; based on what I want to do this week, what do I need to do today; based on what I do today, what I do I need to do right now?" And there's this weird narrowing that happens.' This 'weird narrowing' is the golden nugget that gives the high performer that competitive edge. Some might call it the unfair advantage, but it's simply the ability to follow a simple process of reverse-engineering a goal down to identifying what the most important next step is. One thing at a time.

Committing to one thing isn't easy. In fact, it's downright difficult. We are wired to seek out opportunities, and we often find the allure of a quick win or a shiny object too hard to resist. Personally, I know the challenge of sticking to one task and not jumping from one thing to the next. In business we often come up against the inability to double down on our most valued priority. Focusing on the trivial many over the vital few is not conducive to great outcomes.

How can we say this with such conviction? In 1906, Vilfredo Pareto observed that 80 per cent of Italy's land was owned by 20 per cent of the population. Management consultant Joseph Juran took Pareto's principle and popularised it, calling it the 'Law of the Vital Few'. I recall a long conversation with the manager of one of the world's greatest sports teams, who said that the edge his team had was largely due to its ability as an organisation to 'focus solely on the critical few'.

A commercial real estate company once asked me to help it elevate the performance of its salespeople. It was one of my most exciting projects, as it became clear that they had only one issue: a focus problem. They collectively struggled to focus on where most of their business came from. A small number of customers and a set of specific behaviours brought them 80 per cent of their revenue. When we ran the numbers, this equated to 21 per cent of their customers that brought in the lion's share. Yet the majority of their team efforts were focused on chasing the other 79 per cent of customers, who only generated 20 per cent of their revenue. This same scenario plays out across so many other fields.

Plain and simple, the 80/20 rule states that the relationship between input and output is almost never balanced. I can't reinforce the importance of this law enough: by identifying and focusing on the most productive 20 per cent of our activities, we can achieve greater results with less effort.

In my experience, only a small percentage of people are able to truly commit to focusing on the 20 per cent of activities that drive their biggest outcomes. I'd be confident in saying that roughly 1 per cent of people stay truly focused on what's most important. Are you a 99-percenter or a one-percenter?

What makes a one-percenter

You're a 99-percenter if you identify with the following:

- I'm really busy.
- Most of my action items are 'urgent'.
- I can't stay on top of my emails.

- I complain quite often about people, processes and systems.
- I'm a multitasker with a capacity to juggle many things.
- I'm a yes-person.

You're a one-percenter if you can say of yourself:

- I empower others to work independently without micromanaging.
- I set aside blocks of time for admin and email.
- I don't have a to-do list, I simply focus on my priorities.
- My work is aligned with my purpose.
- I'm deeply focused rather than 'busy'.
- I'm happy to say no to things that distract me from my mission.

Whatever you do, be a one-percenter. The success planning method later in this chapter will help you get there.

The success planning method: an introduction

To reverse-engineer your dream outcome and then make a plan to bring it to life, you'll need a system. A method. A framework. Call it what you like, you'll need something solid to help you do the work each day. I have a simple approach for my clients, it's the success planning method.

Here's an example of how one of my clients, Bill, applied it. For ease and relatability I'll base it on a revenue goal, but it could just as easily be a sporting goal, a team outcome, a health result or anything else that's meaningful to you.

Bill told me he wanted to be in the 'million-dollar club'. He had only ever written $400k in commissions annually, but he really wanted to see if he could supercharge his income. He was gung-ho, ready to run fast and hard at his goal by working harder and longer. But we paused. We took the time to get clear on *why* this seven-figure income goal was important to him. We identified what it would feel like and look like when he achieved this monumental personal goal.

Importantly, we explored what the roadblocks or obstacles might be that would get in his way. He admitted that the thought of planning months and years ahead was somewhat overwhelming. There were so many options and opportunities that he felt frozen. This is often one of the greatest handbrakes on human performance, the silent one that sits in our head and renders us motionless. Procrastination sets in when there are too many moving parts. But getting clear on his MINS (most important next step) made all the difference for Bill.

Bill looked back at his past actions that got him to $400k and assumed he simply had to work twice as hard to reach a million. But the fact was, there aren't enough hours in the day for someone who's already working hard to double that. So instead of looking back, we cast our view forward, to what his life would look like in five years.

Slowing things down, getting radically clear and defining how it would look and feel at the endpoint allowed Bill to approach his El Capitan differently. He reverse-engineered the process and wrote a plan of what he needed to focus on month by month for the entire year. He stepped back from his goal of $1 million in revenue in 12 months. He simply identified what his actions and processes should be, starting with the end in mind.

I've provided below the steps we worked on to help him make his goal a reality. These steps are unique to Bill, but my hope is that they will provide some context for you to create your own plan.

Month 1: Clarity & Client Profiling
- Define my ideal clients (who are the decision-makers I need to connect with?).
- Review past deals to identify the most profitable types of transactions.
- Create a refined client-outreach script tailored to high-value prospects.

Month 2: Referral Engine & Relationship Building
- Contact all past clients to reconnect and ask for referrals.
- Schedule coffee meetings with key industry players (lawyers, accountants, developers).
- Send personalised follow-ups to nurture existing leads.

Month 3: Lead Generation Acceleration
- Commit to making 20 high-value prospecting calls per day.
- Launch a monthly market update newsletter to position myself as an expert.
- Attend and speak at two industry networking events.

Month 4: Expanding Marketing Reach
- Create a LinkedIn content strategy (weekly market insights, case studies and success stories).
- Partner with a digital marketing agency to improve online visibility.
- Start hosting monthly real estate webinars to attract new leads.

Month 5: Process Optimisation & Efficiency
- Identify and automate repetitive admin tasks.
- Hire a virtual assistant to handle research and appointment scheduling.
- Engage with the CRM system to track leads, deals and follow-ups more effectively.

Month 6: Bigger Deals, Better Negotiation
- Study past high-value transactions to refine my negotiation tactics.
- Shadow a top-performing broker to learn advanced deal-closing techniques.
- Start targeting larger commercial properties and corporate clients.

Month 7: Pipeline Management & Follow-Ups
- Ensure every lead has a structured follow-up plan (calls, emails, meetings).
- Set weekly accountability check-ins to track progress toward revenue targets.

- Review and rework deal strategies for any stuck or slow-moving prospects.

Month 8: Personal Brand & Industry Authority
- Pitch myself as a guest expert for industry articles.
- Host an exclusive VIP client appreciation event to build loyalty.
- Create video content showcasing my top success stories.

Month 9: Increasing Closing Rates
- Fine-tune my deal-closing scripts based on past successes and objections.
- Work on handling objections more effectively through live role-play training.
- Experiment with new closing techniques to improve conversion rates.

Month 10: Scaling & Leveraging Networks
- Expand my referral network by forming strategic partnerships.
- Explore co-listing opportunities with other top agents to gain access to larger deals.
- Offer incentives to past clients for introducing new business.

Month 11: Prepping for the Final Push
- Revisit all open deals and accelerate closing efforts before year-end.

- Launch a final marketing blitz to engage last-minute clients.
- Review lessons learned and identify gaps to refine next year's strategy.

Month 12: Reflection & Momentum for the Next Year
- Assess what worked and what didn't, adjusting the plan for continuous improvement.
- Reward myself for milestones hit, reinforcing motivation.
- Set new, even bolder goals for the next 12 months.

We didn't stop there. We brought it back to his goals and actions for the week, and then the day. Here's an example of what one of his weeks looked like for Month 3: Lead Generation Acceleration:

Monday: Prospecting & Pipeline Planning

- **08:00 – 09:00 → Market Research:** Review commercial property trends, new listings, and sales reports.
- **09:00 – 11:00 → High-Value Calls:** Reach out to 20 potential leads from my database.
- **11:00 – 12:00 → CRM Updates & Follow-Ups:** Track conversations, set next steps for warm leads.
- **13:00 – 15:00 → Prospecting Walkthroughs:** Visit properties and evaluate potential listing opportunities.
- **15:30 – 17:00 → Networking Prep:** Organise talking points for this week's industry event.

Tuesday: Building Relationships & Marketing Content

- **08:00 – 09:30 → Client Outreach:** Send personalised check-ins and follow-up emails.
- **10:00 – 12:00 → Industry Networking Coffee Meetings:** Meet with potential partners (developers, investors, legal teams).
- **13:00 – 14:00 → Content Creation:** Write LinkedIn post sharing a market insight or success story.
- **14:00 – 16:00 → Social Proof Work:** Gather client testimonials and case studies for marketing.
- **16:00 – 17:30 → Webinar Planning:** Prepare slides and materials for an upcoming real estate webinar.

Wednesday: Deep Prospecting & Presentations

- **08:00 – 10:00 → Outbound Calls to Business Owners & Decision-Makers**
- **10:30 – 12:00 → Cold Outreach Strategy:** Review data from prospecting and refine approach.
- **13:00 – 15:00 → Property Tours & Client Meetings:** Showcase listings to serious buyers.
- **15:30 – 17:00 → Negotiation Role-Play:** Practise handling objections and improving deal conversion.

Thursday: Strategic Deals & Thought Leadership

- **08:00 – 09:30 → High-Impact Client Meetings:** Focus on warm leads and closing deals.
- **10:00 – 11:30 → Follow-Ups & Proposal Writing:** Send proposals to potential buyers/investors.

- **13:00 – 15:00** → **Speaking Engagement or Podcast Guest Spot:** Position myself as an industry leader.
- **15:30 – 17:00** → **Networking Event or Real Estate Association Meeting**

Friday: Review, Optimise, and Future Planning
- **08:00 – 09:00** → **Weekly Performance Review:** Evaluate deal progress, prospect responses and sales pipeline.
- **09:30 – 11:00** → **Client Check-ins:** Reconnect with top prospects and warm leads.
- **12:00 – 13:30** → **Team/Partner Lunch:** Strengthen relationships within my referral network.
- **14:00 – 16:00** → **Process Optimisation:** Identify bottlenecks and refine sales strategies.
- **16:30 – 17:00** → **Plan Next Week's Strategy**

Saturday/Sunday: Recharge

By the end, Bill had a gameplan for today, tomorrow and beyond. If he followed that plan, from then on all his actions would bring him closer to his desired outcome. Was it simple? Yes. Was it easy? No. At times he got distracted, tired, stressed, worried and confused. It sounds like he was being human, like the rest of us. But because he had a plan, because he knew where he was headed and why he was headed there, and because he had a roadmap to guide him, he could always get back on track. He had his very own success plan.

At the six-month mark, he was nowhere near his seven-figure halfway point. Things might have looked a little doubtful at this stage, but he stayed the course. He kept refining his focus and stuck to the plan. To do this, he simply identified his most important next step. Essentially, every day he reminded himself that the best place to start is at the beginning. He didn't get ahead of himself. One foot followed the other, slowly but steadily. By developing the weekly and monthly practice of reflecting on his actions, inactions and outcomes, he'd developed a colossal competitive advantage. Busy people don't often see the merit in slowing down to take stock, but self-evaluation is the seed of self-mastery.

Getting into the 11-month mark, he was still a fair way off his million-dollar goal, but he had significantly surpassed his previous personal best of $400k. At this point, Bill realised that there were many factors outside of his immediate control that he was spending a significant amount of time trying to influence. For the last month, he doubled down on controlling the controllables.

I'll never forget it. I was driving home on 16 December when I received a call from Bill. It was just a few days before he wrapped up the calendar year and I knew he'd be ringing with an update on the goal he'd set. The elation in his voice spoke volumes. He told me delightedly that he had surpassed $1 million in take-home commissions by a few dollars and with a few days to spare. It's a moment I cherish.

I was so proud of him. But more importantly, *he* was proud of himself. He'd 'knocked the bastard off' as Sir Edmund Hillary declared after summiting Everest. Bill is every bit as inspiring as the great explorers of the world, to me at least. He'd set an unreasonable goal, cultivated massive amounts of self-belief and crafted a simple plan to get there. When the going got tough, he stuck to his plan. When it looked like he'd miss the mark, he committed to consistency. Bill is an example for us all that anything is achievable when you are clear on your outcome, your actions and your consistency. Let's go one step further to distil it into a simple sentence: Great things are possible when you pinpoint your one thing. Bill's one thing was 'Having high-value conversations with serious buyers, sellers, and referrers.' Great outcomes are not reserved for the gifted. They are available to anyone who shows up consistently and continues to start each day with their most important next step.

Keep focusing on your one thing

Keeping to your main thing is your one and only commitment if you want to move towards your highest potential. We touched briefly on your MVP (most valued priority) in Chapter 1. Now it's time to integrate that simple tool to full effect.

Before you craft your very own success plan, let's take stock of some of the key habits that Bill said influenced his outcome most:

- Get radically clear.
- Start at the beginning.
- Take no shortcuts.

It's not complex. Simple things, done consistently. Bill felt that those three habits were the most important and essential to achieving his million-dollar goal. Plenty of high performers don't reach their goals in their desired timeframes, and that's perfectly normal. But lacking a success plan will ensure that you lack a successful outcome. Success needs a plan, so let's craft one in the next principle.

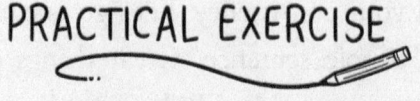

THE SUCCESS PLANNING METHOD

Earlier in the book you got radically clear on your vision. Let's bring it to life with this final exercise – arguably the most important in the book.

The success planning method is an incredibly simple system for bringing your desired outcome to life. This pragmatic system is my own approach and has been informed by mentors, coaches and thought leaders over the years. I've always been conscious that complexity kills execution, so my mission is to distil planning down to something that reduces friction.

First, we will identify each component, and then I'll show you how you can keep your plan front and centre – so you don't get caught in procrastination.

Before we jump in, you need to know there are five phases to success planning:

1. **Envisaging**, where you'll take time to get clear on your five-year vision (5YV).
2. **Planning**, where you'll handcraft your twelve-month gameplan (12MG).

3. **Mapping**, where you'll devise your measurable action plan (MAP).
4. **Stepping**, where you'll create your Sunday success steps (SSS).
5. **Executing**, where you'll define your most valued priority (MVP) for the day.

1. Envisaging: Your five-year vision (5YV)

In the envisaging phase, we start with the end in mind. You already identified your El Capitan and your 10- to 20-year goal in Chapter 1. What might a five-year stepping stone look like? It should be achievable but bordering on the unreasonable. If you need motivation, please know that more than 1000 studies have shown that setting specific goals results in better performance and motivation than setting vague goals. I will never tire of saying that vague goals lead to vague results. If you only do one thing today, get radically clear.

Grab your journal. In one sentence, define your desired five-year milestone and the date, five years out from now, that you'll accomplish it.

This simple format might help:

By [insert month and year], I will have achieved/ reached/accomplished [insert specific and measurable outcome].

It needs to be radically clear and sublimely simple. The more noise and fluff you add, the more confusion you'll create. An ideal example that comes to mind is a client who identified that he wanted to be in the world champion All Blacks rugby team within a specific five-year timeframe, and he did it in even less time. Another wanted to be financially retired within five years, and he reached his outcome in just a few years. Avoid getting too heavy on details. The less you say, the more powerful it becomes. One sentence is your goal.

2. Planning: your 12-month gameplan (12MG)

In the planning phase, we set goals that are further out than a year or two. It can seem a long way off, so we tend to lose sight of the end game and get distracted by the noise. That's often why people flip-flop on their goals and ambitions. A Forbes study found that people who describe their goals in specific written form are as much as 1.4 times more likely to be successful than those who don't. This means that if you write your goals down, you're 40 per cent more likely to succeed than somebody who doesn't write them down. I like those odds. And so do the high performers who outplay their competitors.

Let's tap into something that will enhance your competitive advantage. Here's a powerful cognitive phenomenon: people exhibit better memory retention and recall of information they've created themselves than of information they've simply read or received passively. This 'generation effect' is highly relevant when it comes to goal setting. When you write down your goals, you engage in active cognitive processing that requires you to think deeply about what you want to achieve. This process often involves you visualising what you're writing down. This means you're simultaneously reinforcing the memory through multiple sensory inputs: visual (seeing the words), cognitive (thinking about the wording) and kinaesthetic (writing the words).

According to research, writing by hand is also better for memory and learning. When something is as important as your life or career goals, you'd be mad not to write them down given that's going to help you achieve them more effectively. You are literally keeping them front and centre in your brain.

If you want to maximise your commitment to your goals, write them down and send them to a friend. Researchers in the US found that sending written commitments to a supportive friend resulted in significantly higher rates of goal achievement than just writing down actions and keeping them to ourselves. This suggests that public accountability adds an extra layer of commitment, increasing our likelihood of success. So decide on who you will share your 12MG with and follow through.

Now for practicalities, for which you'll need your journal. You've identified your 5YV, so let's work back to what year one will require of you. Simply step backwards from year five and ask yourself, 'Where do I need to be at the end of this year to be on track for my five-year goal?' Take the time to write down the options you have, the different possibilities and the various pathways you can take to get there. Then whittle it down to one succinct sentence that defines the desired milestone and the date by which you will accomplish it:

By [insert specific date 12 months from now], I will have achieved/reached/accomplished [insert specific and measurable outcome].

You now have a totally unfair (well, I think it's very fair) advantage over those people who resort to setting a New Year's resolution. A long-term examination of New Year change attempts showed that after one week, 77 per cent of people maintained their resolutions, but it dropped down to 55 per cent at one month, 43 per cent at three months and only 19 per cent at 24 months. By actually writing your goal down, you're already a step ahead of the masses.

3. Mapping: your monthly measurable action plan (MAP)

In the mapping phase we get to that 'weird narrowing' that Jay Papasan spoke of. It's a logical approach, even though common sense isn't always common practice. Let's do a one-percenter – one of those small behaviours that separates the one-percenters from the rest. Grab your phone. You should already have an appointment on the last day of each month for your WMI check-in (from Chapter 1). Either edit that appointment to include your MAP or make another appointment alongside it. This half-hour slot will be your monthly mapping commitment, the time when you'll take stock of what you've achieved in the month that has just passed, and get clear on your MVP for the month ahead.

In the same way you went from your 5YV to 12MG, you're now bringing it right down to a one-month goal – your measurable action plan (MAP). Simply put, you need to define what your specific goal is for the month ahead. It won't take long, just a little bit of thought and putting pen to paper (or stylus to tablet). My intention is to give you a colossal competitive advantage over your competitors, peers and opposition. The clients I coach who operate in the rare air of their industries all have this competitive advantage. It's the edge that keeps them at the top of their game. What is it? Simply knowing their priorities and regularly writing down their goals. It seems too simple, too obvious. But it's often the simplest things, hidden in plain sight, that we so often fail to see or do. To create incredible outcomes, do the simple things well, consistently over the long term.

Write down your MAP in your journal using this simple sentence:

> By the end of [insert upcoming month] I will have achieved/reached/accomplished [insert specific and measurable outcome].

Looking to the future and what's possible is one of the foundational pillars of positive psychology. But if we don't take stock of how things have unfolded in the past, we lose out on valuable learning opportunities. If you're taking time each month to plan your goals and actions, then it's equally important to take a moment to reflect on the month that has been. Most people equate excellence with busyness. Never mistake activity for productivity. Slowing things down and asking yourself powerful questions will help keep you sharp and allow you to cultivate that competitive edge. An important part of forward movement is stillness. Sitting still long enough to reflect on lessons learned helps high performers move forward more effectively.

Self-reflection is the seed of self-mastery. Self-evaluation leads to self-awareness. And self-awareness is critical for success in life, business or sport. In her book *Insight*, organisational psychologist Tasha Eurich writes that 95 per cent of people think they're self-aware, but only 10–15 per cent truly are. What makes someone self-aware? Eurich notes that people who focus on building internal and external self-awareness and who ask *what* instead of *why* can learn to see themselves with more clarity.

The *Oxford English Dictionary* defines self-awareness as 'conscious knowledge of one's own character and feelings'. In a world that moves a million miles a minute, how can we slow down long enough to develop consciousness about our character and feelings?

To become more self-aware it's critical to understand and label your emotions effectively. I recall the late broadcasting legend Larry King telling a story about his first day on air. He was so nervous that when he turned down the volume of the song and turned on his mic he couldn't speak. He repeated this off and on for four full minutes. Eventually he spoke: 'Ladies and gentlemen, good morning. This is my first day on radio. I've been sitting here scared to death and you've been hearing music go up and down. But I wanted to tell you that I was scared to death because all my life I wanted to be in radio.' From that point onwards, he said, he was never nervous again. He'd labelled how he felt and it took the power away from the emotion. Many years later, a study into 'affect labelling' explored how naming our emotions can help manage distress. It found that the technique works well on reducing stress, regardless of when we do it. It works well in extremely difficult conditions such as public speaking, exposure to fears like spiders or viewing disturbing images, all of which can trigger strong emotional responses.

Larry was well ahead of his time, and his valuable insights reinforce how important it is that we take the time to acknowledge our feelings and regularly make time for self-evaluation.

Here are three questions I would encourage you to explore each month in your journal:

1. What went well?
2. What didn't go so well?
3. What did I learn about myself or others?

This simple practice will allow you to slow down long enough to draw out valuable lessons and distinctions. And it will shape the month that follows in an empowering way.

4. Stepping: your Sunday success steps (SSS)

In this phase in the success planning method you simply outline your essential steps for the week ahead. It's time to break your MAP down into smaller chunks, which are defined in days. Take time out each Sunday to identify what your outcome for the week ahead looks like and then define your MVP each day.

Step 1: Distil your aim for the week

Write down what you want to achieve by week's end, using the same simple sentence structure as for the other success planning phases:

> By the end of this week I will have achieved/reached/accomplished [insert specific and measurable outcome].

Step 2: Identify your MVP

Write down your most valued priority as an action or step for each day of the week.

This example from one of my clients who was on the PGA Tour shows what his week looked like in the build-up to a major PGA event:

> By the end of this week I will have shown up each day fully rested, prepared and focused on the job at hand. I will have kept the main thing as the main thing.
>
> Monday: I will get clear on the course: strategy, challenges and opportunities.

Tuesday: I will do the reps at the gym, eat well and get a great round in.

Wednesday: I will meditate, meet my mental skills coach and stay relaxed.

Thursday: Game day. I will focus on being fully prepared with the simple things.

Friday: I will learn from yesterday and improve by 1 per cent.

Saturday: I will focus on one hole at a time.

Sunday: I will stay calm and focused on my MINS (most important next step).

As you can see, at no point does he talk about winning. He wins his fair share of PGA events but sometimes falls short. The preparation on his more consistent weeks is centred around the controllables – keeping it simple and getting the job done.

Here's another example of the SSS at work. A client of mine, Judith, is a doctor, a mum and a loving wife. Her life can be chaotic at times, with a hundred things competing for her time and energy. She can often find things overwhelming and all-encompassing. When she takes the time to identify her SSS, though, she says she has much more control over her week. She also says that she feels much more accomplished when she focuses on her priorities. Here's one of her journal extracts:

By the end of this week I will have been fully present for my patients while being present and loving for my kids outside of work hours. I will have enjoyed a date night with Ryan and made it to Pilates three times.

Monday: 5 am Pilates session. Prepare my week, patient by patient.

Tuesday: Full focus on my patients, no distractions.

Wednesday: 5 am Pilates session. Admin and paperwork.

Thursday: Dinner and play date with the kids and their cousins.

Friday: Bring my best energy to work. Date night with Ryan.

Saturday: 9 am Pilates session.

Sunday: No digital devices and a day of family joy (oh, and do my SSS for the next week).

Judith kept it simple and remained committed to specific outcomes. You can do this too. If you don't already have a planning process, start today.

5. Executing

It's nice to have a plan, but when it comes to high performance in life or business, things have to get done.

Action is the only solution. By executing our SSS, we take daily action towards our desired outcome.

Each and every day, when it comes to executing what's required of you to accomplish your goals, you get to choose whether you ripen, grow and flourish ... or rot, decay and go backwards.

Show up. Don't obsess over breaking records. The highest performers I've ever met simply report for duty. It's hard to show up day after day, which is why most people don't bother doing it. By simply showing up each day with a singular focus on executing your MVP, you'll be a one-percenter. It's not about being a masochist and beating yourself to a pulp. By choosing to show up consistently with a radically clear vision and a desire to get better, you will gradually elevate yourself into the rare air of high performance in whichever endeavour you choose.

This last phase of the success planning method is essential. Some talk a big game regarding their plans, visions and dreams. Few *walk* a big game with their daily commitment to the grind of executing their plan.

Take the high road to high performance. Take the stairs, not the elevator. Choose the hard path. Doing the small things with pride and focus allows us to achieve the big things.

First thing each day, be sure to answer this question in your journal: What is my most valued priority today?

You'll notice that it's not plural. It doesn't require you to make a to-do list. It's simply asking you to choose the one thing that will have the biggest impact on your forward trajectory towards your desired outcome. Here are a few examples from different clients:

- My MVP today is to put my running shoes on after I get out of bed.
- My one thing today is to be fully focused with my partner.
- My most valued priority today is delivering a confident speech.
- My priority today is to get the admin and paperwork completed.
- My MVP is to work on my project for eight hours.
- My MVP is to simply enjoy lunch with my friend.

You are now equipped with the success planning method, a one-percenter tool. It's up to you whether you integrate it into your life.

Principle 27: The best place to start is at the beginning

Keep it simple and start. Don't wait until you have a full day of uninterrupted time to plan your future and map out a plan for reaching your goals. If you haven't already done so, grab an empty journal (or even a piece of paper) and turn back to page 25 and begin. As I mentioned, be sure to start with the end in mind. Knowing your destination will inform all of the micro-decisions and actions that will get you there.

Take No Shortcuts

We all know what needs to get done, yet too many of us struggle to get to work. Having a plan is crucial – it's the difference that makes the difference. It removes the need to rely on motivation to get going – it gives you a clear roadmap to follow. So even on those days when you're feeling tired or flat, you just check your MVP and aim to do that one thing. What gets scheduled gets done. If you decide to take a shortcut with success planning, you'd better get comfortable with subpar outcomes.

* * *

High performance is yours for the taking. But it's a habit, not a birthright. You cultivate high performance by choosing to get clear on what's most important. The extraordinary people I've coached and interviewed are just ordinary people who have pursued the principles of high performance and made them into habits.

My hope is that you've done the work in your journal as you've made your way through the book. If you have, I'm confident that you're the one-percenter who will take my high-performance principles and actually integrate them into your life. You have my deep admiration. The journey won't be easy, but nothing great ever gets delivered on a silver platter. Get radically clear on what you're after in life and work, then supercharge your BS to give yourself a shot at greatness. Take the time to get clear on why you do what you do. Become the high performer who taps into intrinsic motivation and does the work day in and day out. Your greatest priority must be to focus on your priorities and embrace the reality that high performers take no shortcuts.

I look forward to hearing about your story. Your vision. Your triumphs. Your struggles. And your high-performance life.

It's time to get out there and lead your life on purpose.

Reader's Guide

This guide is designed to help you integrate the principles of high performance into your daily life. Whether you're a leader, athlete, entrepreneur or someone striving for personal growth, this guide provides actionable steps, reflection prompts and practical exercises to align your actions with your goals. It's not just about reading – it's about doing.

Use this guide as a companion to the book, revisiting it regularly to reflect on your progress, refine your focus, and stay committed to your vision. By engaging with the exercises and questions, you'll develop clarity, discipline, and the habits needed to achieve your El Capitan – your ultimate goal. This is for anyone ready to take no shortcuts and lead their life on purpose.

The book is your roadmap to a high-performance life, built on seven timeless habits derived from coaching, mentoring, and interviewing elite performers across industries.

Grab a journal to document insights and jump onto that QR code to complete the high-performance rituals outlined in each chapter.

Habit 1: Get Radically Clear

Summary

Radical clarity is the foundation of high performance. High achievers possess a crystal-clear vision of their goals, unshaken by distractions or societal expectations. This chapter emphasises the importance of playing the long game, aligning values with vision, and focusing on what truly matters.

Reflection Questions

- What does your personal vision of success look, feel and sound like?
- Are your current goals influenced by societal expectations or your true passions?
- What long-term goal inspires you to stay committed despite challenges?

Action Steps

- Write down your "Altair" – a guiding star for your life's purpose.
- Conduct a WMI (What's Most Important) check-in using the seven pillars: Heartset, Health, Personal Growth, Relationships, Wealth, Joy and Career.
- Identify your top five priorities and rank them in order of importance.

Habit 2: Supercharge Your Belief Systems

Summary

Beliefs are the foundation of high performance. They shape how we perceive the world, make decisions and take action. High performers cultivate empowering beliefs, rewire limiting ones and use visualisation to align their mindset with their goals. This chapter explores how to identify, challenge and transform belief systems to unlock potential.

Reflection Questions

- What beliefs about success, failure, money or happiness might be holding you back?
- Who are the five people you spend the most time with, and how do they influence your beliefs?
- How can you use visualisation to reinforce your goals and self-belief?

Action Steps

- Rewire limiting beliefs by identifying them and replacing them with empowering alternatives.
- Practise daily visualisation of your goals using all five senses to create a vivid mental image.
- Create a Personal Victory Journal (PVJ) to document your wins and reinforce self-belief.

Habit 3: Lead Your Life on Purpose

Summary

Purpose is the emotional fuel that sustains high performers through challenges and distractions. While passion is for personal joy, purpose is outward-facing, rooted in contribution and service to others. This chapter explores how aligning your purpose with your Altair and El Capitan creates clarity, resilience and fulfillment.

Reflection Questions

- What is your personal 'why', and how does it connect to your long-term goals?
- Are you prioritising work that truly matters to you and aligns with your purpose?
- How can you ensure your daily actions reflect your purpose?

Action Steps

- Use the seven levels deep exercise to uncover the core reason behind your Altair.
- Write a purpose statement that resonates deeply with your goals and values.
- Keep your Altair, El Cap and purpose visible to guide your decisions and maintain focus.

Habit 4: Multiply Your Motivation

Summary

Motivation is the fuel that sustains high performers through challenges. This chapter explores the interplay between intrinsic and extrinsic motivation, the role of hormones in driving action and the importance of clarity in maintaining focus. By understanding and mastering these elements, you can cultivate the desire needed to achieve long-term success.

Reflection Questions

- What intrinsic motivators drive you to pursue your goals?
- Are your current habits supporting or hindering your motivation?
- How can you align your daily actions with your long-term vision?

Action Steps

- Identify your two dominant drivers and assess if they align with your goals.
- Implement two lifestyle habits (eg better sleep or exercise) to enhance focus and motivation.
- Regularly revisit and refine your intrinsic motivators to stay aligned with your El Cap.

Habit 5: Do the Work

Summary

Discipline is the cornerstone of high performance. This chapter focuses on mastering the inner domain to achieve external success, refining self-talk to empower action and prioritising what truly matters. By setting boundaries and eliminating distractions, high performers create the focus needed to achieve their El Cap.

Reflection Questions

- Are your daily actions aligned with your priorities and purpose?
- What negative self-talk patterns can you reframe into empowering inCANtations?
- Where do you need to set boundaries to protect your time and energy?

Action Steps

- Practice daily inCANtations to rewire your mindset and amplify discipline.
- Use the high-performance triad (Purpose, Priorities, Activity) to structure your focus.
- Identify and enforce boundaries to eliminate distractions and maintain clarity.

Habit 6: Focus on Your Priorities

Summary

High performers achieve success by focusing on their priorities, particularly their health and well-being. This chapter emphasizes the importance of creating empowering habits, taking your MEDS (Mental training, Exercise, Diet, Sleep), and understanding the neuroscience behind habit formation. By mastering habits, you can predict and shape your future outcomes.

Reflection Questions

- What habits are currently holding you back from achieving your El Cap?
- Which area of your MEDS needs the most attention?
- How can you use triggers to establish empowering habits?

Action Steps

- Conduct a MEDS assessment and focus on improving your lowest-scoring area.
- Identify three habits that align with your El Cap and use the habit loop (cue, routine, reward) to establish them.
- Replace disempowering habits by eliminating triggers and starting small with new, empowering actions.

Habit 7: Take No Shortcuts

Summary

High performance is not about quick wins or shortcuts, it's about consistent, deliberate action. This chapter emphasises reverse-engineering your goals, starting at the beginning, and focusing on your most important next step. Success planning, as outlined in this chapter, is a practical framework for achieving long-term outcomes through clarity, discipline, and execution.

Reflection Questions

- Are you clear on your five-year vision and how it aligns with your daily actions?
- What is your most important next step (MINS) to move closer to your goal?
- How can you simplify your focus to prioritise the vital few over the trivial many?

Action Steps

- Use the Success Planning Method to reverse-engineer your goals from your five-year vision down to daily MVPs (Most Valued Priorities).
- Commit to showing up every day, even when motivation wanes, and focus on executing your plan.
- Avoid distractions by saying no to anything that doesn't align with your mission.

Acknowledgements

To Caroline, Finn and my wider family – thank you for your love, patience, and unwavering belief in me. Your support made this journey possible, and you remind me daily of what truly matters.

To the many mentors, teachers, and leaders who have shared their wisdom with me – your insights have shaped not just this book, but my life's work. Your lessons continue to inspire me and I am forever grateful.

A special thanks to Alex Hedley and the HarperCollins team for helping refine and bring this book to life. Your expertise has been invaluable, and the end product is stronger because of you. A big shout-out to everyone who offered their insights and thoughts on the finer details of the book.

To the incredible leaders, teams and high performers I've had the privilege of working with – your stories, challenges and victories have made this book richer. Thank you for trusting me with your journeys and allowing me to be part of your pursuit of excellence.

To the remarkable individuals who shared their stories on my podcast – your insights, wisdom and generosity have helped shape the ideas in this book. And to those who lent their name in endorsement – your belief in this work means more than I can express.

And to you – the reader – thank you for taking the time to invest in yourself and your growth. High performance is a journey, and I hope this book serves as a valuable tool in unlocking your full potential. The world needs more people striving to be high performers, and I'm honoured to be a small part of your story.

References

James Laughlin, *Habits of High Performers*, podcast

Michaéla C. Schippers and Niklas Ziegler, 'Life Crafting as a Way to Find Purpose and Meaning in Life', *Frontiers in Psychology*, 13 December 2019, https://www.ncbi.nlm.nih.gov/pmc/articles/PMC6923189/pdf/fpsyg-10-02778.pdf

Nelson Cowan, 'The Magical Mystery Four: How is Working Memory Capacity Limited, and Why?', *Curr Dir Psychol Sci*, 4 May 2010, https://www.ncbi.nlm.nih.gov/pmc/articles/PMC2864034/pdf/nihms167613.pdf

'Bobo doll experiment', *Britannica Online*, https://www.britannica.com/event/Bobo-doll-experiment

Maria Richter et al, 'Do words hurt? Brain activation during the processing of pain-related words', *Pain*, 2010, Vol 148, Issue 2, pp 198–205

BL Fredrickson, *Positivity: Top-Notch Research Reveals the 3-to-1 Ratio That will Change Your Life*, Three Rivers Press, 2009

Gerry Leisman, Ahmed A Moustafa and Tal Shafir, 'Thinking, Walking, Talking: Integratory Motor and Cognitive Brain Function', *Frontiers in Public Health*, 25 May 2016, https://www.ncbi.nlm.nih.gov/pmc/articles/PMC4879139

Carmine Gallo, '3 Daily Habits of Peak Performers, According to Michael Phelps' Coach', *Forbes*, 24 May 2016, https://www.forbes.com/sites/carminegallo/2016/05/24/3-daily-habits-of-peak-performers-according-to-michael-phelps-coach/

Martin R Huecker et al, 'Imposter Phenomenon', *National Library of Medicine*, https://www.ncbi.nlm.nih.gov/books/NBK585058/

Tom Bilyeu, 'If You Want to Completely Change Your Life in 7 Days, Watch This! David Goggins', *YouTube*, 2017, https://www.youtube.com/watch?v=78I9dTB9vqM ('Cookie Jar' method at 25:40)

KE Weick, 'Small wins: Redefining the scale of social problems', *American Psychologist*, 1984, Vol 39 Issue 1, pp 40–49. https://psycnet.apa.org/record/1984-25682-001

James Laughlin, 'A Former Criminal's Leadership Lessons with Duro Oye', *YouTube*, 2024, https://youtu.be/D6jjUAol7Wg

Scott O'Neil, *Be Where Your Feet Are*, St Martin's Essentials, 2021

Eddie Jaku, *The Happiest Man on Earth*, Pan MacMillan, 2020

Koichiro Shiba et al, 'Purpose in life and 8-year mortality by gender and race/ethnicity among older adults in the US', *Preventive Medicine*, 2022, Vol 164. https://www.sciencedirect.com/science/article/abs/pii/S0091743522003590

Board on Population Health and Public Health Practice, Institute of Medicine, 'Roundtable on Population Health Improvement – Lessons from the Blue Zones', 8 May 2015, *National Academies Press*, https://www.ncbi.nlm.nih.gov/books/NBK298903

Jason Redman, *Overcome*, Center Street, 2019

Alice Law and Mo Gawdat, *Unstressable*, Pan Macmillan, 2024

Gary Keller and Jay Papasan, *The One Thing*, Bard Press, 2013

Greg McKeown, *Essentialism*, Crown Currency, 2014

References

Aimal Khan et al, 'Three-Dimensional-Printed Models and Shared Decision-Making', *JAMA Network*, 3 June 2025, https://jamanetwork.com/journals/jamanetworkopen/fullarticle/2734064

Steven W Cole, 'Loneliness, eudaimonia, and the human conserved transcriptional response to adversity', *Psychoneuroendocrinology*, 2015, https://pubmed.ncbi.nlm.nih.gov/26246388/

Amanda MacMillan, 'Why Do I Get Sick After Endurance Events (and How Can I Avoid It)?', *Outside*, https://www.outsideonline.com/health/training-performance/why-do-i-get-sick-after-endurance-events-and-how-can-i-avoid-it/

Stacey M Schaefer et al, 'Purpose in life predicts better emotional recovery from negative stimuli', *PLoS One*, 13 November 2013, https://www.ncbi.nlm.nih.gov/pmc/articles/PMC3827458

Angelina R Sutin et al, 'Purpose in life and stress: An individual-participant meta-analysis of 16 samples', *Journal of Affective Disorders*, 15 January 2024, Vol 345, pp 378–85, https://www.sciencedirect.com/science/article/abs/pii/S0165032723013459

Angelina R Sutin, Martina Luchetti and Antonio Terracciano, 'The Benefits of a Sense of Purpose in Life for Healthier Cognitive Aging: Commentary on Sense of Purpose as a Potential Buffer between Mental Health and Subjective Cognitive Decline', *Int Psychogeriatr*, 2022, Vol 34, Issue 12, pp 1015–17, https://www.ncbi.nlm.nih.gov/pmc/articles/PMC10195084

Harvey R Colten and Bruce M Altevogt, 'Sleep Disorders and Sleep Deprivation: An Unmet Public Health Problem', National Academies Press, 2006, https://pubmed.ncbi.nlm.nih.gov/20669438/

Arlener D Turner, Christine E Smith and Jason C Ong, 'Is purpose in life associated with less sleep disturbance in older adults?', *Sleep Science and Practice*, 2017, https://sleep.biomedcentral.com/articles/10.1186/s41606-017-0015-6

Paula Thomson and S Victoria Jaque, 'Personality and motivation', *Creativity and the Performing Artist*, California State University Press, 2017, https://www.sciencedirect.com/science/article/abs/pii/B9780128040515000123

Kendra Cherry, 'Intrinsic motivation: How internal rewards drive behavior', https://www.verywellmind.com/what-is-intrinsic-motivation-2795385

SCHEDULE ME FOR YOUR NEXT KEYNOTE EVENT

JAMES LAUGHLIN

#1 International Best-selling Author
Seven-Time World Champion
Global Keynote Speaker

As a sought-after keynote speaker, James has transformed not only elite athletes and billion-dollar CEOs but entire teams — empowering every team member to embrace personal mastery, adaptability, and high-performance habits. His proprietary frameworks are designed to cut through complexity and give people the clarity and tools to achieve extraordinary results.

What sets James apart is his lived experience of winning against the odds. From leading an underdog team of Kiwi musicians, to a history-making world championship, to serving as the mental skills coach for professional athletes and teams, he brings a pragmatic, proven approach that resonates across industries and cultures.

Beyond the stage, James hosts the *Habits of High Performers Podcast,* where he draws insights from global icons — from Fortune 500 CEOs to world leaders. His message is clear: high performance isn't reserved for a few — with the right mindset and tools, every person can elevate their game and contribute to sublime results.

> ❝
> We had an exceptional day with 70 CEOs from YPO focusing on the power of connection and peak performance. James did an outstanding job and we all really got immense value. –YPO

KEYNOTES THAT INSPIRE AND CAPTIVATE

TOPICS:

High Performance Leadership

Habits of High Performers

Embracing a
Possibilitarian Mindset

How Great Teams Thrive
in Uncertain Times

AUDIENCES:

Small Business
Corporate
Military
Government
Education
Health
Real Estate
Tech
Wealth/Finance
Well-being

SCHEDULE JAMES LAUGHLIN

To inquire about scheduling James Laughlin to speak at your next event, please contact the Gray + Miller Agency at info@graymilleragency.com.

James was fabulous, the team are still talking about the impact he had and the key takeaways. Very practical."
–NZ Trade and Enterprise

LISTEN TO MY PODCAST

Habits of High Performers Podcast, on the Apple podcast charts. Hundreds of episodes. James decodes how the world's best, perform at their best on field and off field.

Guests include:

Christopher Luxon, Prime Minister of New Zealand
Rick Stengel, former managing editor of TIME magazine
Hamish Kerr, gold medal Olympian
Zion Armstrong, Former president of Adidas North America
Jamie Pennell, SAS war hero
Nabeela Elsayed, former COO of Walmart Canada
Daniel Pink, best-selling author of *Drive*
Mo Gawdat, former CBO of GoogleX
Rachel Hunter, supermodel
Ellie Norman, CMO of Formula E

Connect with me at: jjlaughlin.com

COACHING

**Apply for coaching at:
jjlaughlin.com/coaching**

I intentionally keep my coaching personal and focused, working with only a select handful of leaders and high performers each year so I can give each person the time, attention, and depth they truly deserve. Over the years, I've had the privilege of coaching government leaders, billionaires, professional athletes, and driven entrepreneurs — people operating at the highest levels who still want to sharpen their edge and grow. Because that level of commitment goes both ways, I work by application only, ensuring the partnership is the right fit and we can do meaningful, transformative work together.

James

Representing a community of authors whose books have collectively sold hundreds of millions of copies, the founders of The Gray + Miller Agency launched Maison Vero, a professional publishing house that partners with rising authors to bring their thought leadership to the world. Our representation covers every aspect of thought leadership, including U.S. senators, governors, and ambassadors, billionaire founders and entrepreneurs, researchers, academics, scientists, consultants, practitioners, social influencers, C-suite leaders, adventurers, professional athletes, artists, and creators. We partner with thought leaders and world changers like you who have a story to tell. By bringing decades of professional expertise to our clients, we are charting a new path in a timeless industry that transcends publishing norms, transforming powerful thoughts into impactful books that inspire minds, ignite hearts, and open doors.

Visit maisonvero.com to view our growing list of authors, or to submit a proposal for publication consideration.

Follow Maison Vero for insight and inspiration on social media:

 MaisonVero   MaisonVero   MaisonVeroPublishing

For information about special discounts for bulk purchases, please call (949) 333-4872 or email info@graymilleragency.com.

Maison Vero is a partner brand of The Gray + Miller Agency, a speaking, literary, and talent consortium. For more information on the talent represented by The Gray + Miller Agency, or to bring any of our thought leaders to your organization or live event, please visit our website at **graymilleragency.com**.

www.ingramcontent.com/pod-product-compliance
Lightning Source LLC
Chambersburg PA
CBHW020246010526
44107CB00002B/129